The Ugly Side of Being Beautiful

Charity Majors

PUBLISH

The Ugly Side of Being Beautiful
Copyright 2017 by Charity Majors
www.CharityMajors.com

WIPublish
A Division of Women Ignite International, Boise, ID
www.womenigniteinternational.com

Printed in the United States of America

Table of Contents

Dedication	5
Acknowledgements	7
Foreword	9
Introduction	11
Shedding Light on the Problem	13
What the Heck is REAL Beauty?	17
Low Vibes	18
Put on Your Mud Boots	37
A Package That Matches the Contents	51
Monkey Bars vs. Selfie Sticks	57
Sticks and Stones	65
Gifts and Talents	75
Bring on the Arrows	89
Why, Yes, I'll Have Another Bottle of Wine	101
A Magic Wand Life	109
References	116
About Charity Majors	117

Dedication

To the lover of my soul, the one that has formed me, fashioned me, and is so intimately close that He knows the numbers of hairs on my head. He knows my flaws, my mess ups, my hang ups, the good and the bad, and He still extravagantly loves me. The one who has called me, for such a time as this, Jesus Christ. Thank you.

To the amazing souls I get to share this life with: the ones that draw out the best in me, keep me grounded, make me laugh every day, and keep me on my toes.

My husband, Chris: Thank you for always believing in me and encouraging me to go for it - whatever "it" may be. Next to every strong woman is an equally as strong counterpart, and I am grateful that you and your strength are beside me. I love you more today than ever, and there is no one else in the world I would rather adventure through this life with.

My son, Judah: You are my buddy, my partner, and my little love. You are so special to me, and you are one of the only ones who has listened to my heart from the inside. You are the reason I want to be who God called me to be…so I can be an example to you, because I believe you can change the world.

To my daughter, our sweet baby girl, who was only meant for heaven: I can't wait to hold you in my arms. Thank you for sharing your sweet spirit with me, if only for a short while. You have changed me in more ways than I will ever know.

You three are my world, and I love you endlessly.

To my parents, who gave me the loving foundation of who I am now believing I am, who always saw the best in me, and have been my biggest fans. I hope to be the type of parent that you have been to me. Thank you for living out a beautiful example of God's unconditional love, grace, and favor.

To my future self, the one who draws me to pursue the dreams she has already accomplished, the one who has journeyed through the fear I now face, and the one who gives me glimpses of what it's like - the lives that will be touched, the difference that will be made, and how fierce the fire is within me. Thank you. I will see you soon.

And to every woman who, like me, has felt like they were never enough or sometimes "too much," I see you. I feel you. I have been in your shoes and sometimes still wear them. We've got work to do. We can do this. We must do this, because our light, soul, and purpose is here for such a time as this.

Acknowledgements

To my Women Ignite Tribe: Your love, friendship, encouragement, business knowledge and strategies, and the fact that we get to be on mission, together, is how I always dreamed it could be. You are the walking, living, breathing realization of those dreams and that we can have a world where women champion other women in the most beautiful way. From this grateful heart, thank you.

Thank you to the WIPublish team, Director and Editor, Terilee Harrison, and Book Cover Designer, Trevor Allen: You helped me bring this book and my story to life. You challenged me to think bigger, and you drew out the best in me. Thank you for being an integral piece to this beautiful puzzle.

To my MaxGiving family: Thank you for believing in me, my message, and for showing it through your actions. Words could never express my gratitude, and I have no doubt this is just the beginning of what's to come.

Foreword

I have had the honor to speak to the Mrs. Idaho contestants over the years, and I love to scan the crowd and try to pick the winner. I am looking for that contestant that has the best energy, the one that shines from the inside out. This is when I first met Charity Majors. She was different. She radiated beauty on so many levels. Yes, she was beautiful, but so much more. She was beautiful from the inside out - from her smile, from her passion, from her love for everyone she meets. Over the years, I have loved watching her shine and constantly work on all things in her life to share it with as many people as she can. She inspires me.

Charity's *The Ugly Side of Being Beautiful* and BeYOUty Revolution is impactful, powerful, and something we all crave. We need to work on the full person, and Charity shows us the way! We all struggle with something... People are messy. Is it your self-confidence, which in turn hurts your exterior beauty? Or is that you are only focused on external beauty and you need a gut check? Or are you struggling with the ugly side of being beautiful? If the answer is yes, this book is for you. Keep reading and get ready to shine. Charity has that effect on people!

The Ugly Side of Being Beautiful is right in line with my first book, *Better Human: It's a Full Time Job*. We are all far from done and need to work for it by reading, growing, and pushing ourselves. We all want to win. We all want to shine and become the best version of ourselves.

We've got work to do.

Let's go,

Ronda Conger
National Speaker and Award-Winning Author of *Better Human, Better Thinking, and* soon to be released *You Go First*

Introduction

This book is an experience... Get ready...

This book is meant to be more than words on a page and stories of tragedy to triumph. It is meant to be an experience and a resource that not only offers you, the reader, inspiration, hope, and tools to implement, but ways that you can begin to offer that same hope, life, and light to others. Within its pages you will find inspirational quotes that are meant to be a "pay it forward." If a quote resonates with you, take a photo of it and blast it out on your social media so that you can begin to share life and light into the hearts of others. In this book, you will also find website addresses with resources, and links to songs. These web resources contain special messages, videos, recordings, and tools exclusive to the readers of this book. Be sure to have your phone or computer handy so you can get the messages at the right time as you go through the book. The included links to songs are meant to get you out of your head and into your heart. Music has a special way of doing that, so take a moment to slow down, close your eyes, and listen.

I do reference God within some of my stories. I want you to know, I am by no means, pushing my personal beliefs on you. I invite you to fill in what whatever word works for you when I reference God, Creator, etc.

Grab your favorite cozy mug, get comfortable in your favorite space, and get ready to be inspired, challenged, cry, laugh, think, journal, and grow. We are in this together... Are you with me? Here we go...

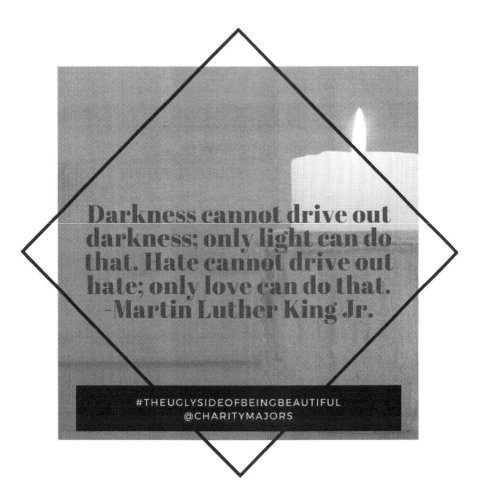

Darkness cannot drive out darkness; only light can do that. Hate cannot drive out hate; only love can do that. -Martin Luther King Jr.

#THEUGLYSIDEOFBEINGBEAUTIFUL
@CHARITYMAJORS

Chapter 1
Shedding Light on the Problem

This book is meant for those of you who have carried shame around the damage you received for looking a certain way. It is meant to bring a voice, validation, and shed light onto something that has been in the shadows for far too long.

It's the ugly side of being beautiful.

This topic isn't usually brought up because it seems "insignificant." The problem doesn't seem like it's "big enough" to actually talk about.

And that's part of the problem.

This topic is hidden. Stuffed away. Brushed under the rug. Deemed "not important" because other people have "bigger problems" in their lives.

Some people experience "cannon-ball" size wounds and other people experience "bullet-size" wounds. But wounds are wounds. Death by a thousand cuts still hurts. No matter the size of a wound, it hurts. One thing I've learned is if there are enough "bullet-size" wounds throughout someone's life, the emotional damage and scarring can be just as painful as a "cannon-ball" size wound. Bullet after bullet after bullet hurts just as much as one big "bang".

This story may seem insignificant to some, and if it seems insignificant to you, this book is not for you (and you also may be a part of the problem). No offense, because I, myself, am part of the problem, too…

Even as I type this, my brain still tries to tell me that this story isn't worth telling. That it's not a topic worth shedding light on. That people will think I'm stupid for even bringing this up. That I am alone in feeling this way and no one else will understand. It tells me that people will laugh at me, gossip about me, and ask, "Who does she think she is?" They will make fun of me, and in the end, my vulnerable and open heart will be hurt. But that's how I know this is a topic that needs light shed upon.

The more your brain tries to talk you out of something, the more you need to lean into that fear and "do it afraid." I've learned throughout my life, that when I use fear as a guide and move into the resistance, the greatest reward, passion, and purpose awaits me on the other side. As I share the stories within this book, please understand that risking "exposure", mine as well as those who have been brave enough to share their stories for this book, it's still scary, but we are doing it anyway.

Knowing that the greatest rewards await you on the other side of being true to your soul and walking through your fears, I want to invite you to join in the experience and conversation with us. Sharing your stories, your mistakes, your lessons, your failures, and your hurt is scary. It exposes someone in all their weaknesses in a world that expects you to stay strong. It reveals your flaws; it blows open the door to your heart, and it shows what goes on behind the perfect social media highlight reel. Sharing my story exposes me and my "junk" (which, my recovering people pleaser side is desperately trying to talk me out of writing this and pushing the save button). #justbeingreal

The more real I become and the more I walk through my own fears and trust my God given purpose and intuition, there are things I learn along the way. If there's one thing I've learned, it's that anything in your life that causes you to dim your light needs to be brought out into the light, talked about, released, and forgiven. **Then** you can grow from it. Even the seemingly "little wounds." These were the wounds that caused me to dim my light. Cut after cut, jab after jab, they hurt my heart and caused me to shrink back, to dim my light, to play small, and to turn my "too-much" of something into not enough. These are wounds that others receive that cause them to dim their lights, to play small, to feel like you are not enough and the way you were made was a mistake.

This book is meant for those of us who have carried shame around the damage we received for looking a certain way. It's meant for those of us who have tried to step into our beautiful God given purpose, and ugly things have happened. It is meant to bring a voice, validation, and shed light onto something that has been in the shadows for far too long.

It's #theuglysideofbeingbeautiful

Chapter 2
What the Heck is REAL Beauty?

On the surface, I am 5'10" with long blonde hair, brown eyes, clear skin, and a lean body. As an outgoing introvert, (yes, that's a thing), I am friendly, I have no problem leading a workshop or speaking in front of people, I can be quiet at times, and need my alone time when I am running on empty. I smile – a lot (my dad said I "came out smiling") – "I like smiling. Smiling's my favorite." (See the movie "Elf" if you aren't sure what I'm talking about).

I tend to give others the benefit of the doubt (sometimes to a fault). One of my top 10-strengths in Gallup StrengthsFinders is Positivity, so I tend to see the best in others, find the good in any situation, and I love to encourage people. I also get this strength from my mom - I'm pretty sure her number one strength is Positivity. We have both been told that we live in "Positivity-La-La Land" (which was not meant to be a compliment), and finally, I'm okay with that. It's better than being a resident of "Debbie-Downer-Ville" if you ask me. But that's another story for another chapter.

I genuinely and wholeheartedly love all people. Like literally, I love people. I love their differences, their similarities, the shapes, colors, textures, different gifts, different passions, different quarks, you name it, I love it. And I love you, especially for reading this book.

I graduated from high school and college with honors. I was a collegiate athlete who still holds school records to this day. I was a fitness and nutrition coach so along with my volleyball career, I am very comfortable in the way I look in spandex. I am a former beauty queen, so I'm also very comfortable in pretty dresses with lots of bling and have learned to do my hair, makeup, and work a stage with the best of them.

As a speaker, author, and lifestyle entrepreneur that gets to be my own boss and work from anywhere, I make more residual income working part-time than some do in their full-time jobs, and I have the honor of teaching others how to do the same. My offices have included beaches in Mexico, parks, my kitchen table wearing sweats and slippers while my kiddo runs around. I absolutely love being an entrepreneur. I say this not to brag, but to share that I have worked really hard, and I have failed more than I have succeeded, but I'm proud of what I've accomplished so far…

My husband is one of the hottest men you will ever see in your life. Combine Gerard Butler and Matthew McConaughey together, and you now have the visual of what my husband looks like (hubba hubba). He was the guy that about 100 girls "just knew" they were going to marry. He is a firefighter (Hello, Mr. July!), he is a musician (I get to go home with the lead singer of the band), and he is the perfect balance of strong and gentle, funny and kind. He supports me with my crazy ideas, we adventure all around the world, he thinks I am most beautiful in my sweat pants and no make-up, he is a great dad, and he makes me laugh every single day. See why they all wanted to marry him? Sorry girls, God had different plans in mind…

My son is as handsome as they come, as sweet as can be, and he lights up whatever room he walks into. If you have ever taken Gallup StrengthsFinder, you'll know what I mean when I say that "his woo is high." (More on this test later).

I became a successful entrepreneur, community influencer, and activist through a lot of hard work and dedication. It's something I am proud of because I truly feel in alignment with my God given purpose when I am leading, loving, and serving others. I also, randomly, chose to do a beauty pageant, fumbled my way through learning about the process, was chosen as the winner, and have had the chance to connect with, coach, and compete with amazing women all over the world. I also learned the best makeup and hair tips known to man, which helps in every area of my life.

From the outside, looking in, there is nothing ugly about my life. It's all beauty, butterflies, and cute babies. #blessed

Being a former Beauty Queen, you may think I'm going to write about beauty hacks, fashion tips, photoshop tutorials, and how to take the perfect selfie. Don't get me wrong. I think all those tools are good to use and if it's right for you, use them to the best of your ability. I'm a firm believer in beauty, inside and out, so be sure to check out the resources page at www.charitymajors.com for some of my favorite tricks and tools to the things I just mentioned. In this chapter, I am talking about a specific kind of beauty. The disconnect between what society says is beautiful, and what we, as human souls, perceive to be beautiful.

This chapter is stemming from what print and media defines as beauty, and the disconnect we, as humans and spiritual beings, **feel** to be beautiful.

Webster defines beauty as: "the quality or aggregate of qualities in a person or thing that gives **pleasure to the senses** or **pleasurably exalts the mind or spirit** (emphasis added); a particularly graceful, ornamental, or excellent quality; a brilliant, extreme, or egregious example or instance."

"The quality or qualities in a person or thing that gives **pleasure to the senses or pleasurably exalts the mind or spirit**." How's that for a definition? Let's break this down and dig a little deeper. Let's start with the senses.

Our five senses consist of sight, smell, taste, feel, and hearing.

Did you know that there are actual physical qualities and measurements that our eyes are drawn to? Things like symmetry in a face, clarity of skin, a healthy body, a smile, and posture? (1)

The media and print magazines clearly utilize what our eyes can see as one of their main ways to convey beauty… hence photoshop or apps filled with filters to give clear skin and symmetrical lines in a face, the ideal image of long luscious hair and a trim waste-line. But what about those of us who aren't a cover model with a photoshop guy sitting in our office waiting to airbrush our every selfie?

On the other end of the spectrum is the "pleasurably exalts the mind or spirit" part of Webster's definition. I created a Facebook poll about what others think makes someone beautiful. Comments consisted of things like "being kind," "gratitude," "helping others," "being happy," and the like. Not one person out of the 100+ comments I received said anything about a physical trait. #Hmmm…

I started to ask myself, if Webster's definition includes the five senses and science shows that we are attracted to symmetry, why is it the Facebook poll responses had nothing to do with physical attributes? And why is it that print media and trending social media applauds and encourages the physical attributes like a thigh gap, long fake eye lashes, a tiny Barbie waste, and puckered lips? (Can we *please* be done with the duck face already? This is being encouraged to the point that teenage girls are injuring their lips by putting them into shot glasses, sucking so hard it breaks blood vessels and their lips swell.)

And why are we (especially as girls and women), so focused on the ugly things when it comes to this beautiful world? We focus on our "not enough-ness." The parts of us we want to change or enhance because of the beauty standards we are bombarded with every single day. Where is the disconnect between what the media says is beautiful and what we truly *feel* and *know* to be beautiful? Where is the beauty that we experience that lies within each and every human being that God created?

Experiencing someone else's beauty (not just perceiving it) goes deeper than just what you perceive with your eyes (and it's deeper than what the media shoves down our throats as their standard of beauty). It has to do with how one's innate self (or subconscious) interprets those physical qualities. Whether you know it (or believe it), your innate self is interpreting data at every moment; over 80,000 interpretations of the world around you at any given moment, to be exact.

Your subconscious mind interprets signals in others like their scent and pheromones, the shape of their body, the health of their smile and teeth and mouth, length and quality of hair and nails, and the whites of their eyes. When someone has skin blemishes, your subconscious interprets that as unhealthy on the inside, and it comes out through the skin. Your subconscious interprets other things like another person's energy or "vibration" they give off. Have you ever been around a "Debbie downer" and felt the need to get as far away from them as possible? Or maybe you've seen a creepy guy and feel like you need to go take a shower and clean off the creepiness? #yeahmetoo Your subconscious picks up on the energies and vibrations of everyone and everything around you. These signals and vibrations are too much for your conscious mind to handle at one time, so all this interpretation happens at a subconscious level – a level you aren't even aware of… until you are.

Now, stick with me here if you aren't the "vibin'" type and let's take you back to science class. If you can remember that far back, you may recall that everything on the planet is made up of atoms. Atoms have either a positive or negative charge. When you pair atoms together, you get the elements of earth. (Remember the Periodic Table of Elements?) Hydrogen (H_2O = two hydrogen atoms and one oxygen atom), aluminum, chromium, and all the other ones I don't remember…

Every cell of your body is paired together with atoms, giving it a certain "charge" or "frequency". The higher the frequency, the more conscious and alive the object is. For example, a plant is made up of all its special combination of atoms and has a higher vibration than my sunglasses, which has its own special combination of atoms that make up the plastic, metal screws, and lenses

Here is another example that you probably have heard of. "Alive food" or raw food is more "living" than cooked, processed, or packaged food. A fresh carrot out of the ground has a higher frequency or vibration than a boiled carrot, and it definitely has a higher frequency than cheese puffs, which are the same color as carrots. Why? Because the boiling water and the heat changed the frequency of the molecules that made up the carrot and it changed it physical properties and vibration. And cheese puffs? Well, let's just say that there is nothing natural or alive about them, especially not the neon orange chemicals that cover your fingers and insides after eating them. Make sense?

#keephangingwithme

There are ways to raise and lower your personal frequency or vibration. Everything that you do, every single day, affects that. Obviously, we all are vibrating. It just depends on what you have put into your body, which feeds your cells, which divide and create more cells that continue to create your body. Is your body made up of cheese puffs and the chemicals in soda or are your cells made up of living foods like greens and herbs and organic ancient grains?

What we put *into our bodies* isn't the only thing that affects the way our body vibrates. How we *move* our bodies also matters. Remember when you learned in science class that a body at rest stays at rest and a body in motion stays in motion? Have you ever experienced the momentum of when you start working out, you are more motivated to keep working out? And isn't the starting always the hardest? It's because of this principal. I encourage you to find exercises, activities, classes, and a lifestyle that encourages you to stay in motion. Movement is one of the best ways to increase your vibration and it's even better when we can connect the body and the mind, like with yoga. #yogiforlife

Besides just how we move our bodies and what we fuel our bodies with, what goes *into our minds* has a huge effect on the energy signals we put out to the world, bigger than you may think, and studies are finally showing evidence of this. If you think about it, #punintended, our brain and central nervous system operates on tiny nerve signals that are electric in nature. Electric. Electricity. Signals. Radio waves. Get the connection and where I'm going with this?

Did you know that certain thoughts and states of mind have different frequencies and that it has actually been measured? States of gratitude, peace, courage, love, abundance and joy vibe at a much higher frequency than states of fear, grief, apathy, anger, shame, and scarcity.

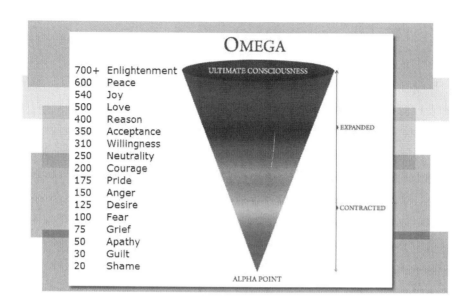

This chart shows the measured vibration frequencies of these states of mind. (2) Now, you may be wondering what this upside-down birthday hat has to do with anything beautiful. This chart and these frequencies or vibrations have to do with how we experience others and how they *experience us*. How their subconscious interprets our personal vibrations and energy. Remember the second part of Webster's definition of Beauty? "The quality or aggregate of qualities in a person or thing that gives pleasure to the senses or **pleasurably exalts the mind or spirit.**"

#vibes. Exalting the mind or spirit. High vibes. Enlightenment (or understanding). Joy. Love. Reason. Acceptance. Willingness (or being open). Courage. Neutrality (seeing things from all angles and being okay with others difference of opinion). Gratitude. Peace. This is where the good stuff is. Where, when we operate from these spaces, others "feel" who we are, and they are captivated by it. We vibrate kindness and love. We give off the energy of peace and clarity and openness and service. That leaves others with a feeling – an experience. They remember it. They like the way they feel around us. They post on a Facebook thread that these qualities and characteristics are what makes a person beautiful. You literally vibrate and radiate true beauty. No photoshop filters, no unattainable standard from print media, no sucking your lips through a shot glass. Just raw, real, radiant beauty, vibrating from every cell in your being, vibrating from your soul. The way it should be.

#Beautiful.

Now that you have a better understanding of energy, there are things that you can do, on a daily basis, that help raise your vibration so that you begin to allow others to feel your highest and best self. These things include meditation and gratitude, clean eating, and removing toxicity from your body, living an active life, and living a life of purpose, in alignment with your purpose.

For ways to raise your vibration and tips to implement them daily, visit CharityMajors.com/BeautifulResources and this Chapter tab.

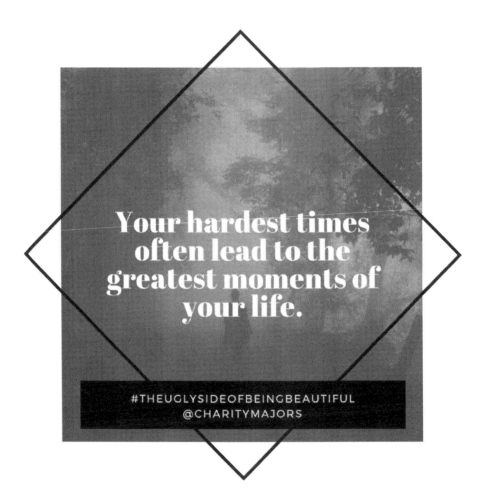

Your hardest times often lead to the greatest moments of your life.

#THEUGLYSIDEOFBEINGBEAUTIFUL
@CHARITYMAJORS

Chapter 3
Low Vibes

But what about the low vibes? The shame? Fear? Apathy? Pride? Anger? Guilt? Grief? What happens when you are coming from a place of these lower vibrations? What happens to your body, your mind, and how does it affect those around you? This is a part of the "head model" of the personal development world that most people try and mantra themselves out of. There is a new understanding – the heart model – that is beginning to take hold, and it includes acknowledging that these feelings exist (instead of pretending they aren't there), and heading straight into the places of our darkness.

In July of 2017, I went through one of the most painful experiences of my life - painful in body, mind, and to the soul level of who I am. I experienced a miscarriage. I was almost 11 weeks pregnant with a little soul, heartbeat, and life within me. This baby was a surprise to my husband and me, but we embraced the adventure with joy, gratitude, and excitement. I was healthy, active, had a flawless first pregnancy, and beautiful homebirth with our son. So, although miscarriage was a passing thought in my mind because "it's always a possibility and that's why people don't post on social media until after 12 weeks," the thought of losing our baby wasn't really on my radar. Until it was. It wasn't supposed to be in the plan for *our* family. Until it happened. Until I experienced much of the process of a miscarriage – not at home in a safe and private place – but in a very public place, with all eyes on me and nowhere else to go.

My husband, Chris, my one-year old son, Judah and my mom (thank God for family who can come along and help take care of a kiddo while traveling) were on a trip. It was a quick little weekend getaway to relax, enjoy the lake and mountains, and reconnect. Little did I know that the bleeding I had started to experience would lead to a trip to a midwifery where the midwife would regretfully tell us that she couldn't find a heartbeat, and this was the start of what she called a "spontaneous loss." In a split second, my heart shattered into a million pieces as I melted into my husband's arms. It wasn't just my eyes and emotions that were crying. It was my heart and soul. The dreams we had envisioned of our little family, the prayers I had prayed over this little life, the hopes and dreams that come along with the gift of a child, all ripped away in an instant with the simple words of, "there isn't a heart beat." Driving back to our hotel with tears streaming down our faces, and the song "It Is Well with My Soul" playing on Pandora, we decided to pack up and catch the next flight home. Within a couple hours, we could be at home in a safe and comfortable place, while I experienced the effects of the miscarriage.

We made it to the airport as my cramping and bleeding increased. We prayed that the 53-minute flight would be short enough so we could make it home. It wasn't. In all of my pain, cramping, and the point of almost passing out, I was trapped on an airplane having one of the worst experiences of my life. Taking trips to the tiny and sterile restroom at the front of the plane, every 5 minutes was humiliating and isolating. Bleeding through my pants, sweating profusely and being in visible pain, I felt shame like I had never known before. The constant looks from other passengers and questions from the flight attendants wondering what was going on seared into my breaking heart. I felt helpless, broken, and trapped. I felt afraid and alone, despite my husband's best attempts to comfort me, hold me, stroke my hair, and get me cranberry juice. All I wanted was to be at home, in our safe place, where I could process the loss of our child in a way that I felt comfortable (or as comfortable as one can be in that situation).

After what was the longest 53-minute flight of my life, we landed and immediately drove to our midwifery center where we received care and compassion throughout the rest of the process.

I was told that physical and emotional healing would be a process, and I should continue to rest. What they didn't tell me was that I wouldn't want to get out of bed in the morning and that I would question God's faithfulness and goodness. What I didn't know was why it happened and what the purpose behind it was. What I didn't know was the fear I now felt, surrounding my perfect and healthy one year old and how my mind would run to the worse case scenarios. Is he going to choke on that food? Is he going to fall and break his neck? Is he going to wake up in the morning? Is someone going to take him from me? What if I can't keep him safe? Am I failing as a mom? Should I read him a book instead of just laying here crying? These made up stories always ended up with him dying, or that I would feel like I was drowning in shame and guilt that there was something wrong with me and my body. I didn't know such dark places existed, but I experienced them with every cell of my body and soul.

I questioned God, I questioned myself, my purpose, the purpose of life, why it's even worth it, and why I was even living. Most of my thoughts began to stem from a place of fear, anger, grief, apathy, and shame. The lowest of the low vibrations, all at once, without any light at the end of the tunnel.

Maybe you, like me, have experienced feelings like this. Shame. The feeling of not wanting to get out of bed. Anger. Lack of understanding. Questioning whether it is worth even living another day. Unfortunately, in this broken world, these deep seeded emotions are an ugly side of this beautiful thing we call life.

It is within our deepest, darkest times and where the most pressure can be applied, that what's on the inside will come to the surface. Within this deep place of darkness, my shame, my anger, my grief, and my brokenness surfaced. Knowing I couldn't go through this alone, (despite my husband's best efforts, and he was *amazing* through the entire process, it's just that his processing and grief was different than mine), I sought help through a grief counselor. I knew that this deep seeded, soul shattering brokenness wasn't something that I could "mantra" my way out of, and I needed professional help. The counselor began a therapy called EMDR, which is a light and sound technique that allows the right side of your brain and the left side of your brain to connect on a high level. This brain connection allows the person having the EMDR treatment to pay attention to the patterns, stories, and body sensations that connect to the tragedy they are processing through.

Through my therapy, I found relief through the process and joy in the pain. I was healing by going straight through my grief (instead of stuffing it, ignoring it, or achieving my way out of it). I also found that a lot of where my feelings of shame and being broken was connected to a lot of the wounds I experienced at other times in my life. The stories I share in this book. This is part of my healing, and it is my hope that through the messiness that I have experienced and the healing that I have intentionally sought out, that it can provide hope and inspiration to someone else who may be in the thick of it. Through processing of the loss of what both Chris and I felt was a little girl, I began to see some light breaking through my darkness. I again began to believe in, and draw upon, not only my family and community, but in my God given strengths. One of my strengths is Positivity, which means that I can find the best in any situation and in any person. I began to, although painfully and I admittedly wanted to just wallow in my bed and not do anything, search for the good in this soul shattering situation. I began to see how the life of my daughter, even though she was only meant for heaven, was a life enveloped in love and the joy that comes with receiving a surprise gift. I began to see how grateful I was for my son and the miracle that he is. I began to see how every single person on the planet is a beautiful miracle. Did you know that there are millions of pieces and parts of DNA and cells and atoms that must perfectly align and come together for life to be sustained? My son is a living, breathing, walking miracle. I am a living, breathing, walking miracle. You are a living, breathing, walking miracle. What a revelation to have! Through this tragedy, I gained a new level of understanding of how every single human is a beautiful miracle and beautiful creation. I began to feel overwhelming gratitude for life and for those around me. I began to process through the shame and the brokenness of my past and take another step into my God given purpose. This is part of that. Sharing the light that comes out of darkness is part of my purpose, and although I will never "arrive," I am stepping forward, in faith, believing that there is a gift in every situation, and choosing to draw out the nuggets of gold, so that I can share them with you.

I want to encourage you that if you, like me, have experienced the brokenness and hurt that one can experience through life, through loss, through abuse, through misunderstanding, through false perception, or whatever it may be, to follow those promptings and trails of hurt, to do the work needed to heal, and to share your story. We all have a story to tell and it can only be told in the way that you can tell it. I invite you to begin to surround yourself with those who will embrace your "too much," and your bright shining light, along with the dark side that we all have. Find those who will draw the best out of you – draw out the high vibrations of love and joy and peace and gratitude, courage and consciousness. And those people or experiences that draw out the lower vibration energies of shame, anger, apathy, etc… those are there for a reason, too. It is meant to be a clue to show you where you need healing, where you can do the work on your heart and soul (and it may take professional help), so that you can begin to offer the same healing and hope for others.

And to those of you who have experienced loss, whether it is a child, maybe it was the loss of a job or a marriage or a friend or hopes and dreams, I invite you to find the gold among the heat. It's within you. It always has been. It's up to us to embrace the pressure of life and develop into the beautiful bright shining light that is within us so that the world around us can be bright and beautiful.

Because darkness cannot drive out darkness. Only light can. Hate cannot drive out hate. Only love can... —Martin Luther King, Jr.

I invite you to take a moment and listen to the song, "It is Well," under this chapter's resources at CharityMajors.com/BeautifulResources. It was an encouragement to my soul that even in the middle of a storm, that God can use everything for good and that it *is* well with my soul. This is also my prayer for you.

Shame for women is the web unattainable conflicting competing expectations about who we are supposed to be. To do it all, do it perfectly, and never let them see you sweat.
-Brene Brown

#THEUGLYSIDEOFBEINGBEAUTIFUL
@CHARITYMAJORS

Chapter 4
Put on Your Mud Boots

Imagine a swamp. Tall trees, tangled bushes, weird smells, creepy sounds, and mucky water that you have to sludge through without knowing what's below the surface. #freaksmeout

Shame and Vulnerability expert, Brene Brown, calls shame the swampland of the soul. (If you haven't seen her TedTalk on Shame and Vulnerability, it's a must watch. I have linked it in this chapter's resources at CharityMajors.com/BeautifulResources). Guess what, Beautiful One? Even though it's not the sexiest of topics, put your mud boots on because we are diving right in with this chapter.

#Shame

I felt like throwing up. I was humiliated. The core of my heart and soul was screaming in pain to hear that my "friend" had publicly shamed me. She had not only socially and publically trash talked me and the new friends I had made, but the entire pageant industry. And it was all over social media for the world to see. I didn't understand. She had been the friend that came with me to try on dresses and cheered me on from the audience. She told me she believed in me day after day, when I decided to compete and as I prepared for the actual competition. She met some of the amazing women I was getting to know and become friends with. Women who were supportive, encouraging, active in the community and fun compared to the stereotype of catty and snobby pageant women. I'll admit, before deciding to join a pageant, I too, had a perception of "pageant girls" and that they were just pretty girls in dresses. After actually joining, getting to know the women and seeing what they are about, I can truly say that they are some of the kindest, service oriented and driven women I have ever met. If you want to challenge yourself to grow, if you want to increase your confidence and beauty – inside and out, and join a supportive group of women, I highly recommend finding a pageant in your area and going for it! It was one of the best decisions I made. I have no doubt you will be greatly surprised at how positively it affects your life.

Speaking of contribution, my "friend" even started to volunteer at an organization I had been involved in because she was inspired by my work in the community due to my involvement with the pageant. She was so excited for me when I unexpectedly won the entire thing. She said she was my biggest fan and knew it would be me. She was proud of me, proud to be my friend, and happy to stand by my side. She knew me, who I was, she knew my heart, my hopes and dreams and that they were coming from a good place.

We had been each other's "person" for the last ten years, and we had been through a lot. We were by each other's side through thick and thin, through finding love, losing love, through business ventures, the girls' nights and the BFF necklaces. We shared our hopes and dreams with each other and always had a lot of fun together. She had stood next to me on my wedding day when my husband and I had said our vows. She was my #bestie. And now this? A public blast of me and "who I had become" in the span of a weekend of a competition - that I was a narcissist, I was selfish, I didn't deserve to win, that pageants were nothing but insecure women vying for the stage and for attention... And "she would never..."

Then it magnified. The #toxin of gossip spread like a cancer. She got together with a few of my other "friends" and unloaded more ammo. Hurtful words. Slander. Name-calling. Backstabbing. It seemed to be a social-media frenzy. Hurtful comments bred more hurtful comments and likes and shares. #unfriended

My heart was crushed. I was hurt. I felt humiliated. I felt attacked - like 100 arrows had been shot right through me. The logical side of my brain said this was a stupid situation and I should just suck it up and move on...that I didn't need her anyways. But my heart didn't understand. I couldn't see where the disconnect was from being encouraged and supported a few weeks earlier to being publicly shamed by my best friend of ten years.

How was I "here" again? I thought this childish stuff was behind me. Weren't we past high school and college? You see, this wasn't the first time this had happened. That's the thing about repeating patterns that show up in your life...they will continue to show up so that you can learn the lesson to a greater depth. There have been other instances in my life where someone has verbally slandered me. Remember the saying, "Sticks and stones will break my bones, but words will never hurt me?" Well, bull-crap to that! Words (the wrong words), are one of the most hurtful things in the world. I have felt the pain over and over, all throughout my life. This was one of my life patterns. Although I was raised in a supportive and encouraging family, I still experienced hurt by people who were either role models in my life or people I was close to and knew my heart, my hopes, my dreams, my flaws, quirks, and were there on good days and bad days. That's why it hurt so bad…

Because I had been told by a coach that he didn't like my personality, I would never play in a volleyball match, I took on the belief that there was something wrong with who I was on the inside. I am a first born, so my natural leadership qualities were deemed as being bossy. I was teased in high school for being in the National Honor Society, so I felt stupid for being smart. Some guys told me I was "too pretty" for them or that I was "intimidating" so the sting of rejection for how I was made dug deep. Being a tall but shy high school girl earned me the title of a B@%$& among other girls. Wearing a ribbon in my hair, while I dominated on the volleyball court, made me too girly for the sporty girls, but being a high-level athlete made me too sporty for the girly girls. I was even hazed and called horrible names, by fellow teammates because I wouldn't shot gut a beer at a party. My positive attitude and ability to see the best in others or in a situation has prompted others to tell me that I live in "Positivity La-La Land" and ride on a magical unicorn and they would rather live in their reality than be near me.

This is where the shame of being beautiful began. And when I say beautiful, I mean the unique combination of personality, strengths, gifts, and looks that God gives someone. #theuglysideofbeingbeautiful is really the attack on who we are and the beautiful potential that lies within us to make the world a better place. I used to think that my looks, my natural gifts of leadership, being smart, and always seeing the best in others – the way God made me – was a mistake. I was tired of other women looking me up and down and giving me the stink eye. I was tired of being "too pretty" for a guy and feeling the pain of rejection. As a people lover, I just wanted relationship – real connections with people who didn't pre-judge me and knew and loved me for me. Because of this desire and the negative feedback I was receiving from the outside world, I began to "dim my light" as I like to call it. I began to downplay my beauty, dress in sweats, I tried a lot of different hair styles and colors that did not bring out the best in me. I hid behind an extra 20 pounds and quieted my people-loving personality. I started to play small.

I dimmed my light so that others wouldn't feel inferior or self-conscious around me anymore. I became an achiever, a do-er, and a people pleaser. I had more masks than a girl has shoes. I was striving to do it all and make it look easy. I've had to keep it together, make it look perfect, keep straight A's, and have my hair, nails, clothes, and makeup look just right. And don't forget the "don't let them see you sweat" (or fart) part of it.

Now, don't get me wrong, makeup, fashion, and the desire to look and feel confident on the outside is a good thing. There are actions we can do that enhance what we are naturally given. We can put on makeup and do our hair and wear trendy clothes and push-up bras (all the mamas know a good push-up bra is helpful for confidence). Those physical actions of enhancing beauty have been a part of human civilization from the beginning of time. Even Cleopatra wore eyeliner and lipstick, jewelry and beautiful garments. And those actions – in balance – are not wrong.

I love a good lipstick and pair of pants that make my butt look good. But it's when we use these actions of external beauty to hide who we really are instead of enhancing them. Shame is hiding behind layers of makeup that is caked on so that no one can see your freckles because you hate them (hiding who you are and how you were made). And yes, I used to do this.

Shame is either hiding in clothes because you are ashamed of your body and how it looks or over-flaunting your assets because you have been taught that is how you get positive interaction and attention with people versus with your personality. So, you mask your personality with over-exposure of your physical assets, almost to draw attention away from who you are and just show what you have. I used to do this, too.

I know what it's like to feel foolish, believing who I was wasn't good enough, smart enough, pretty enough… Or at times I was too much for someone - too pretty, too smart, or too tall. My beliefs, the things that made me, me, were criticized and made me feel like who I was and how I was created, was all #wrong. Gosh, do I know that feeling all too well.

I can't say that I've felt the pain of physical abuse or sexual abuse and the shame that comes along with that, so please understand that I am not downplaying those injustices. These are definitely a part of #theuglysideofbeingbeautiful as well. I can say that movements like the recent social media movement of #metoo, shed light on a lot of darkness about physical and sexual abuse, that has been hiding for far too long. I believe there has been a step towards understanding, freedom, and healing due to sharing those stories. What I can share from personal experience, (and because it's in one of my favorite books that I base my life on), is that I believe there is life and death in the power of the tongue and what is said either speaks life and light or death and destruction.

Even as I write this, my internal monologue (or what I like to call my "inner-critic) is trying to get me to feel humiliation and foolish - to shame me.

"These are all #firstworldproblems."
"These wounds you experience aren't worth talking about."
"They won't care about your story or your message because you are the only one who feels that way."
"No one will listen or care."
"There are bigger problems to worry about like starving kids in Africa."
"Who are you to say this kind of stuff?"
"You're nobody."
"You're not a writer or a psychologist or an expert in any of this."
"You're not smart enough to talk about this."
"Who you are is not enough."

Well, isn't that fun to listen to? Shame comes at us from multiple angles. According to Webster, it can come from others who use shame as a verb or action – "(of a person, action, or situation) make (someone) feel ashamed." Shame can also come from ourselves... from the internal dialogue that resides deep down in our subconscious, that we have somehow attached a belief to an action from somewhere in our past.

Now, there is a difference between shame and guilt, and I believe it's important to know the difference. Shame is "I *am* bad," while guilt is "I *did something* bad." Guilt is "I *made a* mistake". Shame is "I *AM* a mistake". See the difference?

Guilt is about the action while shame is about the person – the being.

In her book, *The Shameless Life: Recognize Your Shame and Overcome It*, Terilee Harrison shares the power in shame isn't what happened to you or what you have done, the power in shame is in what you *think*.

Shame comes from 3 places:

You can feel shame about how you're made. Shame is personal. What you feel intense shame about may be "no big deal" to someone else. You can be you're too tall, too short, too fat, too thin, your skin is too light, your skin is too dark, you're too smart, or you're not smart enough. The list is endless.

You can feel shame from the things others have done to you. A third of the humans walking this planet have been physically abused by others. This is NOT okay. At a minimum, you may have had someone say hurtful words which have stuck with you and caused you to feel shame.

You can feel shame from your mistakes. We all have done things we are not proud of. But sometimes you can feel more than guilt about what you've done, you can come to believe that *you* are bad.

In Terilee's case, she was born with an underdeveloped reproductive tract and came to believe when she was 12 years old that she was different than *all* other girls. Although she looked pretty on the outside, for years she felt ugly on the inside. No one would have guessed how much she didn't like herself. The thing is, what you believe on the inside is what you will manifest on the outside. She felt so unlovable she began to make all kinds of bad decisions in her life. Her low vibes just attracted more low vibes in her life. Thankfully things have changed for her and she is now reaching out to help others overcome their shame.

I believe that bringing #theuglysideofbeingbeautiful to light, as insignificant or as #firstworldproblem-y as it may sound to you or me or our (mainly my) internal monologue, it needs to be brought to light. We can only find things in the dark when we shed light on them, so here I am, flashlight in hand (well, more like a big spotlight – which feels bright and harsh and vulnerable) shining a light on all of my "junk", on my wounds, fears, and insecurities, I'm hoping to give you permission to begin to shine a light on yours, too, so that we can *all* move toward the path of healing and wholeness. I'm also shining a light on these things because I don't believe I am the only one that feels this way. #wearenotalone

I believe other women bury their feelings of not being good enough or being too perfect or being intimidating or bossy because it isn't a "big enough wound" to talk about. Guess what, Girlfriend? #ifeelyou I know what it's like to bury the feeling of not being good enough or being too much or being not pretty enough or being too pretty. I know how you feel when someone says that you are intimidating or bossy or they put you in the category of a shallow dumb blonde and a pretty person with no depth or substance to them because that's just how #prettypeople are - shallow, with no substance.

Here's the thing about wounds... They hurt regardless of the size. Whether you get a splinter in your hand or it is cut with a knife, it still hurts. I sometimes think the small splinter-wounds that go unseen by the naked eye are even more painful than the trauma of a large wound. Because they fester, (and usually multiple splinters get layered on top of each other), they are below the surface, buried in the swampland of shame and and they dig a little deeper with each movement. They can cause serious infection if not dealt with.

There is almost more "grace," forgiveness or understanding for a "knife-size" wound... like, "oh, she was in an abusive relationship so that's why..." or "yea, she was sexually abused when she was younger, so we can let her actions slide..." You can visibly see the wound and scar and so somehow that makes people understand or accept it more. But the "splinter" size wounds – the ones that sound like "#prettypeopleproblems," or "oh you're beautiful, so you don't have any problems," or "you're too perfect," or "gosh, wouldn't it be nice to be you..." Splinters. Splinters that dig deeper and deeper. Splinters that get stacked upon more splinters. Wounds that fester and hurt.

So yes, Beautiful One, whether or not you have experienced splinter size wounds or knife-size wounds, they still hurt. Whether you have experienced 100 hurtful comments about your appearance or about who you are, one traumatic experience such as rape or abuse, it still hurts. Your 100 splinters are still painful. So are mine. And I'm here to validate them. To say that you are not alone, and that your splinters do matter.

They do. They matter a lot. And it matters that we do a little digging to uproot them, so you can heal. Because the magic is found in the healing process. When you are brave enough to venture through the swamp of shame and start your healing process, you give others permission to be brave and seek healing in their lives, too.

Shame is highly correlated with addiction, depression, violence, bullying, eating disorders, obesity, aggression, control, and suicide. Can you think back to times where you have felt any of these negative side effects? Can you follow the rabbit trail even farther and think of where these actions stem from? Think of every time you acted out in a way that stemmed from the deeper issue of shame. For example, if you have dealt with an eating disorder, there may be certain points throughout your life that triggered your beliefs about food and your body. These beliefs took hold sometime in your past – usually childhood. This is called the "root" of the problem.

But there's good news… You can change the way you take on that belief. You just have to do the work and the uprooting that comes with it. It is a process, it takes time, and it never fully goes away, but you can build up a "shame resistance", as Brene Brown likes to call it. For example, when someone used to say something negative about me, I would be devastated. It would hurt me to the core of who I was and send me into a negative tailspin.

Over time, as I began to heal and grow and believe in who I was and grow in confidence in how my Creator made me, negative comments didn't hurt as much. They started to bounce off the armor of my self-worth and the belief that I am not a mistake, that God made me just the way He intended to, that I am enough, I have what it takes, and that I am here for #justatimeasthis

You, too, can build up your armor, but you must first dig out the splinters. The healing of these shame splinters starts with knowing yourself at a deeper level, and loving and accepting who you are and how God made you, despite what anyone else says or thinks because, let's face it, they are dealing with their own wounds, too.

It comes down to believing that your beauty is not a mistake. You are here for such a time as this. You are smart enough, good enough, and you have what it takes. You are worthy, you are loved, and you are perfect just the way you are – flaws and all.

When you can operate from a space of trust and belief in those things, it will reflect in your actions and how you show up in the world. For me, I no longer hide in sweat pants, and I am at home in my beauty and in the fact that I like pretty things. I like the floral prints, flowy-fabrics, pinks and golds, and sparkly things.

I no longer worry that if I wear those things someone is going to say, "I'm too girly" or "I'm prissy" or "too pretty" because I also know that I've got this Zena-Princess-Warrior/Wonder Woman mixed with a Disney Princess vibe and under my pretty floral dress is a big, awesome sword that can chop the Devil's head off. I have also been very intentional about who I have now surrounded myself with. I believe that there are women out there, like me, who believe that we, as women, are meant to live in sisterhood. To live in harmony, grace, support, and love for each other instead of insecure competition that tears down one another. I can even look back at the past friendship I had with the girl that I mentioned before, and I am grateful for it. Through the gaining and losing of that friendship, I learned so much. I learned who I want to surround myself with. I've learned that there is a gift in everything. I've learned more about perception and how people view others based on the wounds they have received from their past. And more importantly, I truly and wholeheartedly hope and pray that she is doing well and loving life and letting her own light shine.

My guess is that you have a similar vibe as me – that Wonder Woman / Zena-Princess-Warrior / Disney Princess / sisterhood vibe - because like attracts like and you wouldn't be reading this book if you didn't have it. My guess is that you, like me, are also here for such a time as this and you have known this, deep down in your heart, for your entire life.

You believe that there is more in store for you…and it's #BIG. Bigger than you may know or care to believe, but there is an inner knowing (whether you like to admit it or not), that tells you that you are here for a special reason. I believe it, and I invite you to begin to believe it, too.

I also invite you to dive into more resources that can empower you to build your shame resilience, own your God given beauty and build your body armor at www.CharityMajors.com/BeautifulResources. You can find the resources under this chapter in the Resources section.

Chapter 5
A Package That Matches the Contents

Now that you have gotten through some of the swampland and understand that you don't have to hide who you are in shame anymore, there are ways that you can accentuate your assets and have the outside match the inside. This is the part where my beauty queen experience comes into play because I think beauty doesn't have to be just on the inside or just on the outside. I believe it is meant to be both. Before we dive into those resources, I'm curious as to whether or not you have ever gotten a drink and thought it was one thing and when you took a sip, it was something completely different? How did you feel? It catches you off guard, right? It is surprising, kind of puzzling and sometimes causes liquid to come out of your nostrils. #thatmayormaynothavehappenedtome Maybe you've experienced this because you are a Coke fan but you were given a Pepsi, and you were just downright pissed. (I've heard this is a very serious offense!) (Side note-I am not endorsing drinking soda of any kind…it's bad for you…seriously though. Stop drinking soda. Remember the chapter about doing things to raise your vibration? Soda does not do that. Your insides will thank me later. #steppingoffsoapbox)

The way that you dress, do your makeup, your hairstyle and jewelry can create the same effects as the wrong drink – the confusion, the being puzzled, the liquid coming out of nostrils #okaymaybenotthatone - if you don't "wrap yourself" in a way that matches who you are on the inside.

Let me explain… Remember how your subconscious picks up on over 80,000 signals at any given moment? Parts of the signals that get picked up happen to be with your appearance. Did you know that you are naturally attracted to things of symmetry, and things that appear "healthy?" This is an innate thing that got passed down from our cavemen ancestors and it's a little concept called "the strong survive." We subconsciously pick up on signals like healthy, glowing skin, thick hair, good posture, muscle tone, and healthy teeth because these things are a window into how healthy our body is on the inside, how able we are to reproduce and keep a species alive.

So, as you can see, not only does having healthy skin, hair, nails and complexion matter, but so does the way we "package" our body. Did you know that there are certain colors, shapes, and fabrics that best fit different personalities? It's true! Think back about the drink analogy...or here's another one to let your brain wrap around this concept. If you had a bag of potato chips, reached in and it was cheese puffs, you would be a little puzzled, right? (I'm not sure why these analogies are using junk food...I don't even eat potato chips or cheese puffs...but whatever...you get the point. Now go eat an apple and drink some Kombucha). #formerhealthcoach #icanthelpit Anyway... You would be puzzled because what was on the inside didn't match the package, right?

YOU are the same way! You have a certain personality and it shows up in your facial features; in the way you express your emotions, how you speak, your expressions, your body language, your posture, etc. And if you are wearing the wrong colors, textiles, fabrics, cuts of clothing, shapes of jewelry, the wrong haircut or color, all this stuff creates incongruency with how others interpret who you really are.

Insert subconscious signals being picked up from someone else – if you wear a color that clashes with your personality, it creates a subconscious signal that the other person picks up that you aren't whom you say you are. There is also a deeper subconscious energy that you will have because you may not feel as confident in what you are wearing or how you are presenting yourself because it feels incongruent – it feels "off."

Have you ever seen a shirt or outfit – either on Pinterest or on a friend or on a hanger – and it looked awesome? You just had to buy it right away? You bring it home, try it on, expecting to feel as awesome as it looked on that random girl on Instagram, but when you put it on, it doesn't give you the same feeling? That's because it may not be something that fits you and your "being." But here's the catch (I know because I used to do this all the time) – I would keep it – with the tags still on – and hang it in my closet and tell myself that I will try it on again another day. Maybe it's just a "fat day" or my hair is off.

A week later, I try it on again, when I am having a really good hair day and still, it makes me feel "blah." I can't seem to get rid of it because of how cute it looked on someone else, so it stays in my closet, with hopes that one day, it will recreate that feeling I had when I saw it on Pinterest, but it goes unworn in my closet and takes up space. And now my closet is overstuffed with clothes that don't bring that feeling of #yeeaaahhguuurrrllll when I put it on, I have a hard time deciding on what to wear because most of it doesn't make me feel great, and my self-confidence goes down.

Have you ever experienced this? I didn't know it traced back to having a closet full of stuff that didn't match my "being." I didn't know there was a way to dress so that it best suited me, my personality, my facial features, and how I wanted to show up in the world (and that it could save me money).

You might be thinking, well gosh. This sounds really complicated. I just want to go to the store and pick something out without having to analyze the color and shape and cut and textile and fabric type. That sounds complicated. I am here to reassure you that once you know your "type" and have guidelines to follow, shopping becomes easier and more enjoyable. It is easier to let go of the clothes that are taking up space in your closet that you hope to wear one day.

It makes it easy to pick out things that best suit who you really are and how you want to show up in the world. Your confidence will drastically increase. Your closet will be less cluttered. You will save time when you pick out outfits, you will save money because you aren't wasting it on buying things that sit in your closet and never get worn. You will be sending off subconscious signals that you are in integrity with who you are. Your package will match the contents. There will be no ugly weird subconscious signaling to your beautiful self.

No more awkward spitting out the wrong drink. No more liquid coming out of nostrils or frowning in puzzlement because you pulled out a different chip from the bag. Just the right message at the right time, in integrity with who you are and how you were made. Which is perfect and beautiful. And for such a time as this…

I invite you to take some time and go through your closet. Sort through the things that you have and if it doesn't "spark joy," as my good friend and author of *Purple Crayon Confidence*, Kayla-Leah Rich, likes to say, then get rid of it. How do you know if something "sparks joy?" It's that outfit or piece of clothing or pair of shoes that when you wear it, you feel like a million bucks and nothing could wreck your mojo. It makes you feel giddy inside. Put it on, feel all the feels, and then as you try on other articles of clothing from your closet, if it doesn't give you those same feelings, out it goes! I like to suggest donating clothes that are no longer serving you to those in need, but if you need the cash to get other articles of clothing that make you feel like a million bucks, then by all means, sell them and go shopping with the cash.

Before you go shopping, or if you are struggling to find which type of clothing best fits you, I want to invite you to take a FREE Energy Profile Assessment on my website. This energy profile assessment will give you an idea of how you were made and which energy matches what fabrics, shapes, colors, textiles, etc. If you want to dive deeper and take the actual course (which is one of my favorites), there is also a discount code so that you can match your contents with your package. Visit CharityMajors.com/BeautifulResources and find the tab for this chapter.

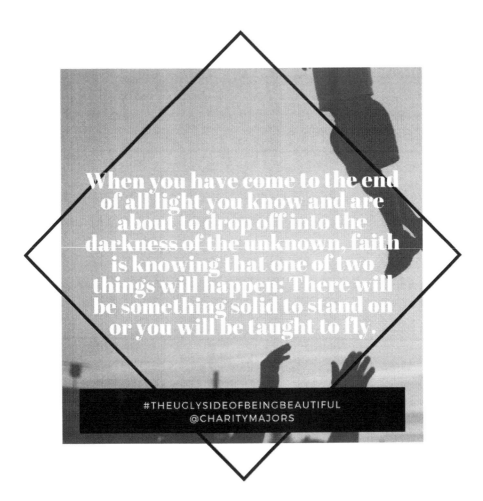

When you have come to the end of all light you know and are about to drop off into the darkness of the unknown, faith is knowing that one of two things will happen: There will be something solid to stand on or you will be taught to fly.

#THEUGLYSIDEOFBEINGBEAUTIFUL
@CHARITYMAJORS

Chapter 6
Monkey Bars vs. Selfie Sticks

I remember it vividly. I was hanging there, legs dangling in the air, my knuckles were turning white, my hands were starting to burn, and the ground was a long way off. "Daddy, but will you really catch me if I let go?" I squealed. "Yes, Love Bug, I will catch you. Even though you can't see me, I'm here, and I won't let you fall."

I was about 5 years old, and my dad and I were at a playground. I had been running around like the carefree happy child that I was (probably dreaming about being in happy la-la land riding my unicorn, or maybe I was a Disney Princess with my super cool warrior sword). I decided today was the day I would go all the way across the big kid monkey bars. One rung after the other, I started to make my way across what seemed to be the longest monkey bar set known to my 5 year old self, but my tired, little hands and fingers could barely hang on for another second. My dad was close by, he heard me calling for him, and he came over. Being the wise man that he is, he chose to use this little playground as a teaching moment. He stood behind me and told me he would catch me if I fell. I couldn't see him, but I could hear him. "I won't let you fall. I promise. You can trust me." I held on tighter, wiggling in fear, and still questioning if my dad would actually catch me or whether I would end up in a full body cast because every bone in my little body would be shattered the moment I hit the ground that was so far away. "Even though you can't see me, trust that I am right here. You can hear my voice. Let go. I won't let you fall."

I couldn't tell if I had mustered up enough bravery to actually let go or if my tired, little hands finally gave out, but I eventually let go. I let go, and I somehow just *knew*, and I fell right into my dad's loving arms, just like he promised.

That day, a life lesson was etched into my little heart. One that I will never forget, and one that I believe shapes who I am today. I learned about trust. I learned to trust not only my dad, but I learned to trust the voice of Truth that lived inside of me. The voice that spoke to my heart and called me, Beloved. The voice that never condemned me, but drew me to a higher standard of myself and called out the best in me. The voice that was typically deeper and quieter than the other chattering voices that I hear in my head, but it was the voice I trusted the most.

There was a time in my life where I began to ignore this voice. I began to shut it out and listen to so many other things around me. I began to listen to the other kids who would make fun of me or pick me last. I began to listen to the coach who told me he didn't like my personality. I began to listen to the voice of the boy who rejected me. The message from the media that said I wasn't pretty enough, perfect enough, or airbrushed enough. I began to listen to the voice of society that said I should just hunker down, find a good job, work for 40 hours a week for the next 40 years, be a good girl, go to church, act like I'm happy and like everything is okay and live in a perfect little house with my perfect little family and cook perfect little dinners. I began to listen to all of the social media chatter that never seemed to slow down or shut up. The posts, the comments, the filters, the best parts of everyone's day, while all I felt like was a failure, not good enough, not pretty enough, not smart enough, and I kept dimming the places where I was "too much" so I wouldn't offend anyone.

I have a feeling I'm not the only one who has experienced this. How does this happen? How have we, as a society, slipped into this mindless existence of scrolling, feeling numb, wasting time, and not living the life we are truly called to live? How do we find our way out of this ugly side of the beautiful world we live in?

Well, it's science...

Studies show that social media gives the same dopamine response as alcohol, smoking, and gambling. Dopamine is the neurotransmitter that signals to the brain a positive response. Epinephrine does the same thing but there is a difference. Dopamine is short lived while epinephrine is a "slower burning" response. It's kind of like a camp fire... Dopamine is the kindling while epinephrine is the log. The log might take a little more to actually catch fire and get hot, but when it does, it burns a lot longer than the kindling and it has a higher function – to put out heat.

Dopamine and Epinephrine work the same way in the brain... Dopamine is meant to only be the kindling when it comes to "igniting" happiness in our brain and Epinephrine is meant to be the longer sustaining sensation of fulfillment, love, and connection. But what happens when, in today's world, most of the love and connection that we are chasing is fueled by the kindling – the superficial connection and rush of Dopamine that we feel when we look at our social media... when I get more likes on a post, when we get good comments on that last selfie we took. When someone shares a good quote that I made up in a new app that I found that has the coolest font and I watermarked it with my @handle? It makes us feel good. It makes us feel popular, liked and significant, right? But only with kindling. Only with the superficial shot of neurotransmitters that burn off quickly, so we search for more. We search for another hit. Another viral post. Another post in the perfect selfie position with an even better filter so that it will get even more likes this time because my duck face was even better.

What's wrong with us? Well, nothing. We are hard-wired to move towards pleasure and away from pain so when we feel the Dopamine hit of "approval and likes and significance and shares and acceptance" from our "friends" (as Facebook has so conveniently labeled them), it fulfills a deeper need that we, as humans, instinctually have and need to survive. The need for connection. The need for love. The need to feel significant, and that we are making a difference in someone's life.

I'll be honest when I say that I am concerned for the younger generations who have grown up with a phone in their hand and a digital friends list that they seek approval from. Over half of teenagers reported having been bullied over social media. One out of ten adolescents and teens have reported that they have had an embarrassing photo taken of them, unknowingly, and it was posted without their knowledge or consent. (3)

And with access to social celebrities who are seeking attention in an unhealthy way and using their influence simply for likes and comments on their duck face photos and revealing breast or booty photos, what type of messaging is the world sending back to these younger generations? I believe it is creating such an unsafe, disconnected, not-accepting, have-to-be-perfect and superficial understanding the world around these children, at a deep subconscious level. I only *hope* that we, as parents/adults/those who have learned a little along the way, have been able to heal our hearts enough to provide them with the depth and the relationship and acceptance and the teachings that failure is a part of life, enough to equip them for this crazy digital world and where it's headed.

When it comes to social media, I believe the problem is that we aren't getting the deeper connection that we need to thrive and to actually be fulfilled and satisfied. It's all kindling. We don't have the deeper conversations with a person face to face, because it's way easier to shoot out a general message in between errands throughout our busy day. It's easier to type out a mean response to a screen and push send than it is to say it to an actual person. We don't have the conflict resolution skills because all we do is delete and block someone out of our lives instead of sit face to face, cry, share our hearts, seek to understand their side of the story, share how we really feel, how we hurt, and offer and receive forgiveness. We only see the perfection, and never the failures. We only see the good times and not the bad. Empathy is at an all time low because we see our friend's kid, a cat video, our aunt's sandwich that she ate for lunch, and a starving child in Africa, all within the same scroll of a finger. We measure our life to Pinterest and the perfect blog photos that we save and pin, hoping that we can clean our kitchen enough to take a decent photo to post. We've lost the ability to truly connect in a world that has never been more connected.

Now don't get me wrong. I'm not saying burn your phone, never get on social media again, move to the mountains, never shower, grow a beard, and live off the land. Shower for God's sake. #showeringisgood Social media can be a great tool to stay in contact with family and friends, to share a message, to support a business, to meet someone from a different part of the world, to raise awareness for charitable organizations, etc. It's also a great place to find a super supportive tribe in a Facebook group, like ours. #shamelessplug

But when it comes to social media, how much is too much, how far is too far and how many mindless scrolls with our finger is too many scrolls? When is the comparison we naturally and constantly do with everyone else's highlight reel and our everyday messy lives enough? When do we stop hiding behind a screen and truly connect with someone, soul to soul? How much of this ugly side of what can be a beautiful tool are we going to stand for? How do we get back to the innocent place of hanging from the monkey bars, falling into a loving community, and trusting the voice inside of us instead of the other voices that are bombarding us from every angle?

I believe the answer to this comes by healing our hearts first, and finding the true connection – the log that burns big and bright, over the kindling – connecting soul to soul, heart to heart, within a tribe that lifts you up and encourages your fire to shine bright. Use social media to find someone that has a similar mission to you, and then create, foster and nurture that connection in real life. Follow the right role models and influencers – the ones that are using their influence to impact people and not just impress them. Create a beautiful space in your home that *you* love, vs. what Pinterest or a blogger says to love. Be intentional about how long you scroll through social media. Set a timer if you need to. If it's the first thing you do in the morning before you get out of bed, leave your phone in another room (yes, yes, I know…it's an alarm clock…well, I suggest just buying an actual alarm clock. They do still have those around). Start a morning ritual of a gratitude journal or exercise…doing the things that will raise your vibration and set the right tone for your day. We cannot lead others if we cannot lead ourselves so once we begin to lead ourselves in the right direction, filling our mind and body with the right things, and listening to the voice of Truth, that's when the log will catch fire.

Then, and only then, can we begin to assist others, when they are ready to be unplugged and set on fire. Oh, and to trust. Trust the voice of Truth inside, that draws you to let go of the things that may be hurting you. To let go of the habits that move you away from the reason you were put here on this planet compared to the habits in your life that move you towards that purpose, and remove the hold on the things you cannot control. Then fall. Fall faithfully into the arms of grace that have always been there and will always be there to catch you. It's the safest place to be.

I invite you to visit CharityMajors.com/ BeautifulResources. Under this chapter, you will find a song that I hope you take a moment to listen to, along with a morning routine.

Chapter 7
Sticks and Stones

I remember reciting over and over, "Sticks and stones may break my bones, but words will never hurt me." But why did their words still hurt? Was I weak? Was I a wimp? I closed my eyes and recited the poem again to myself, "sticks and stones may break my bones, but words will never hurt me." I opened my eyes, hoping that the hurt would magically disappear. But it was still there. The pain. My heart hurt deeply. I wanted to crawl into a hole and never come out.

I had just been told I wasn't invited to play with the other little girls. #rejected #notenough #outcast #weak #alone #inadequate I also felt wrong for feeling hurt because, apparently, I wasn't supposed to feel that way since "words will never hurt me." At a young age, I stacked another brick around my little heart and attached a belief that girls didn't like me, and that I wasn't "enough" (pretty enough, smart enough, nice enough, whatever enough) to be accepted as a part of the group. I attached a belief that it was wrong to "feel" a certain way because of a popular societal belief (or a rhyme in this case).

Even as a teenager and college student, who was constantly in groups of women because I played sports and was considered a "popular girl" in high school, I was still guarded due to little experiences like the one I shared. I would show up to practice, do my job, and go back home, with the excuse I needed to finish my homework or study for a test instead of going out with the girls. When I actually did agree to go out, it was superficial and lacked depth and substance. I was guarded and never got too close. We were surface friends who could go out, have a good time, never dive deeper into our souls and truly connect, and then we would go home.

In my experience, the layering of bricks to guard my heart and the holding people at an arm's length started because I felt like there was an attack on who I truly was and how God made me. What I've found is that #theuglysideofbeingbeautiful is truly the assault on someone's beauty and their true self, and this assault can have many forms. It can be the hurtful words from another child, a parent, a coach, or authority figure. It can be the hurtful words you say to yourself when you look in the mirror or mess up on something. It can come through sexual and physical abuse and the taking of something that isn't theirs to take. It can be the violation and thievery of a beautiful child or woman who is taken and trapped in the sex trade and human trafficking industry.

It can come from the impossible standard of beauty that the media and magazines shoves down our throat and the feeling that you should pick a better filter or airbrush your photos better before you post them. It can be the eating disorder that someone has so that they can meet that impossible standard of beauty or maintain a little bit of control in a chaotic world. It can come from the lack of understanding of different cultures, beliefs, skin tones, and political sides. It can come from the inexhaustible temptation to compare your everyday mess with everyone's social media highlight reel. But where is the truth in that? Where are the authenticity and the real-ness? Where is the human connection in all this surface stuff? Where is the space of healing, where we can connect, soul to soul and truly accept, honor, and celebrate all of our beautiful strengths and differences? Where is the beauty in all of this ugliness? The world is longing for it. Can you feel it? #itscoming

It wasn't until I became an adult that I realized the longing I had to have deeper and authentic connections with other women. I was at a point where I couldn't ignore the feeling anymore, like I had done when I was younger. But the thought of being "more than surface friends" with other women brought up some old feelings. I was scared.

I was scared of being rejected again - of not being invited to "play" with the girls, like I had experienced as a little girl. I was afraid of the feeling that I, for whatever reason they decided, that I didn't fit in. I realized the little girl inside of me still had her feelings hurt and it was holding me back from moving forward. I began to give into my heart and unpack that belief. I had to do the work to remove the bricks I had stacked, and start to heal the little girl's heart within me that felt that way. I went back to those memories, drew out the good lessons I learned from them, and began to disassociate from the pain through visualization techniques. It provided learning lessons and the healing process I so desperately desired. As I began to heal, I stepped out, scared as ever, and joined some women's groups. Not just any groups...groups that resonated with me, the mission I believed in, and the type of women I wanted to intentionally surround myself with. It took some trial and error, but I started to find my tribe. I started to see how amazing women truly are. They were encouraging, supportive, bright, and beautiful. The friendships I began to develop had depth and substance. They were life-giving and soul-nourishing.

It was how I had hoped it would be. It wasn't until I changed my personal belief and narrative around other women that I was able to step out, be vulnerable enough and okay-enough with who I was and how God made me, to surround myself with women who equally wanted to shine bright and see me shine bright. None of our bright lights intimidated the other, and in fact, we encouraged each other to shine even brighter. We were lifting each other up, drawing out the best in each other, and it felt like it's how God intended women to be together. It was, and still is, the dream of sisterhood and tribe I always believed it could be.

Looking back, I still don't understand why we tell kids to recite the little rhymes that are the exact opposite of truth. Yes, sticks and stones may break my bones. AND words can actually hurt a lot, sometimes more than sticks and stones. I have two younger brothers, so I know how bad sticks and stones can feel. And why are we meant to feel wrong for having words hurt us? Do we realize that this is causing a childhood subconscious belief that feeling hurt by words is wrong? #mykidswontbelearningthisrhyme

I finally realize that I am not wrong for having my feelings hurt by the words that someone says and neither are you. You were not wrong for taking another brick and stacking it in front of your heart to guard it because of the hurtful words that came out of someone else's mouth when you were younger. Where these words get dangerous is when you begin to internalize them and believe them about yourself. That you are unlovable, that you aren't worthy, that you are ugly, that you need to be perfect, that you can't show weakness, that my "butt this", and my "fat that".

From those words and beliefs sprout actions. Actions, or a response, can show up in many ways. It can show up as anger, shame, blame, comparison, control, guarding your heart, putting on a fake mask, and never showing flaws so we appear to be perfect. These things move us away from our most authentic and beautiful self.

The beliefs that the ten out of every one hundred women who suffer from anorexia, bulimia, and binge eating that have been internalized can be traced back to childhood wounds and words from others. It starts so small and once the snowball gets rolling, it turns into something much bigger. The psychological factors that can contribute to eating disorders include low self-esteem, depression, and lack of control in one's life, feelings of inadequacy, anger, anxiety, and loneliness. These feelings create patterns within the brain and are caused by distress in one's appearance, body weight, and shape.

This is another aspect of #theuglysideofbeingbeautiful – or the attempt to be beautiful based on a certain standard, expectation, or belief. Eating disorders are usually developed during adolescence and can carry on through teenage years and adulthood if not properly addressed. Being a health coach, having been in the fitness industry and pageant industry, I have known girls, seen girls, and coached girls who struggle with eating disorders.

I haven't personally battled with an eating disorder, but I can identify with the need to control my body, my workouts, and nutrition to look and feel a certain way, especially when the world around me feels out of control. I have seen the effects of the need to control one's body when things feel out of control. I have heard the thoughts that these girls and women think about themselves and how they use food to create a feeling within them. #itsheartbreaking.

When did we forget how divine, how beautiful, and how powerful we truly are?

It is a slippery slope - one that a lot of girls and women struggle with. If you, or someone you know struggles with an eating disorder or addiction, I want to encourage you to seek professional help and begin to trace back to where it started. It may stem from a belief that was attached to an action someone else did toward you or against you. I also want to encourage you to begin to seek the assistance it will take to unpack those beliefs and reframe those thoughts of inadequacy, unworthiness, feeling ugly, isolated, shame, and never enough. Beautiful Girl, you have what it takes, and you were made in the image of a beautiful Creator. There is hope and light for you and your life. You have a purpose, a big one at that.

Those who walk through the deepest darkness usually do. If you are willing to say yes to the journey... It is all meant to be a part of your process, growth, and the mess that make your message your own. The trick is learning to unpack the bricks and layers, to learn and truly own your God given strengths, abilities, and purpose, and be okay when someone throws a dart of a hurtful word at your heart. Your power comes when you turn it into compassion and a deeper love for where that person is at in their journey.

It will take work, it will be hard, and it will be #worthit. It will be worth it because the story of your life is worth telling. It is worth telling those who will follow suit and experience similar things in their life that they have experienced. You will be the one to offer the hope and the belief that there is a light on the other side of the darkness they are walking through. #shinebrighter

I believe that as women, we are being called higher. Being called to more. Being called to own our fierce beauty, power, grace and love in a way that the world has never seen. I want to invite you to take a moment to slow down, open your heart and listen to "You Have Called Me Higher" by Sons and Daughters (visit CharityMajors.com/BeautifulResources and find the song under this chapter).

You are good enough to be someone else's beacon of light. You are brave enough to step into the mess of your message and begin to shine a light on the dark places of your heart so that you can shine even brighter. You are beautiful – all of your strengths, all of your body, all of your heart and all of your soul. You are fearfully and wonderfully made and every hair on your head is accounted for by a God that is not far off out in the universe, but a God who is close to your side. You are worth loving fiercely by yourself and by others. Your journey, your heart, and your life are worth it. God does not make mistakes and He definitely didn't make one when He made you.

But the choice is yours - to own it and take on the challenge or to stay where you are. My hope and prayer is that you choose to head straight on into the fear, into the darkness, into the mess, and do the work. I am here, we are here, as a tribe of women, to lift you up, support you, challenge you, encourage you, and shine bright with you. You don't have to go alone. No sticks. No stones. Only words of life and light and a sisterhood to draw out the best in you. Come, join the tribe…you will fit right in and feel at home.

Find the link to join my FREE Facebook Group at CharityMajors.com/BeautifulResources. You belong.

The Ugly Side of Being Beautiful

Our Greatest Fear

It is our light not our darkness that most frightens us.

Our deepest fear is not that we are inadequate.

Our deepest fear is that we are powerful beyond measure.
It is our light not our darkness that most frightens us.
We ask ourselves, who am I to be brilliant, gorgeous, talented and fabulous?

Actually, who are you not to be?
You are a child of God.
Your playing small does not serve the world.
There's nothing enlightened about shrinking so that other people won't feel insecure around you.

We were born to make manifest the glory of God that is within us.

It's not just in some of us; it's in everyone.
And as we let our own light shine, we unconsciously give other people permission to do the same.

As we are liberated from our own fear,
Our presence automatically liberates others.

—Marianne Williamson

Chapter 8
Gifts and Talents

I hadn't eaten spicy food so what I was feeling wasn't indigestion. It was a feeling deep down in my soul and I couldn't shake it. I was so discontent at where I was that something needed to change. Something drastic needed to happen. But why now? Why all of a sudden? I had loved what I was doing as a personal trainer and health coach. I loved making a difference in people's lives and helping them. I loved seeing their "ah-ha" moments when they would notice changes happening in their body and in their lifestyles. If I loved it, why was I so discontent?

I like to call it the "divine discontentment". The moment you realize that you are evolving beyond what you are currently doing and you are being drawn to the "what's next" in your life. But where was this feeling coming from? I was making a difference in people's lives. Why wasn't I satisfied with it? Why did I want more? Was I being selfish in wanting to make a bigger difference? In wanting my life to count for more? Was I making it about me? Who was I to want to impact the world?

I like to attribute this feeling to the core and soul need that we all have to be *significant*; the knowing in your core that what you are doing matters and that what you are living for will outlive you. I like to attribute the reason it took me so long to do anything about it was because of the internal chatter that kept me stuck where I was.

Who was I to want to impact the world?
What did I have to say that anybody would listen to?

Who did I think I was?
An author who has something to say that people will listen to? A beauty and soul expert?
A selfish person who wanted to be on stage?
Why should people listen to me?

It was conversations just like that that kept me from moving forward. Truth be told, I wasn't an author, but why couldn't I be? Truth be told, I wasn't an expert inspirational speaker, or workshop facilitator, and that's okay. Truth be told, I had a lot of work to do on me before I could share this with you. #andthatsnolie

Growing up, I remember what it was like to have a home phone and to have all my friend's numbers memorized. I remember what it was like to leave a message on an answering machine or walk to my friend's house to see if they wanted to play. I remember what it was like to finally get our first home computer and have dial-up internet. I still remember the sound it made when it started up and the fact that we couldn't use our home phone while someone was on the internet. I remember the first time we got a cell phone and when it finally got caller-ID so we could see who was calling. I remember when Facebook started and some of us even resisted because who had time to be on that face-space-thing to see when people were going to the gym or eating avocado toast…who cared? #idoloveavocadotoast

Now days, it seems like anything goes. People post about their vacations, their kids, their work, and how they can't wait for the weekend. They post pictures of their cats, tand heir feet in the sand while on vacation to make the rest of their friends jealous that they aren't on vacation, too.

There are videos that go viral, articles that get shared, inspirational quotes, and passive aggressive rantings that go on. There is a lot of information and a lot of noise. How do you sort through the noise online? More importantly, how do you sort through the noise in your head? Your head is filled with more information than you know what to do with. It's almost like there are millions of old school computers all logging into the internet at once. Reeeeeeeeewwwwwwaaaaaaaaaaaaaaaaa…

You have news at your fingertips, tweets that share the latest reality TV show drama, Instagram to show your fancy latte with a heart on the top of it, and Periscope to have random Q & A's with anybody around the world. There are more personal development books, podcasts, blogs, and vlogs than you have time to read, listen to, and watch.

Yet why are so many of us still stuck either in the *divine discontentment* of what has become our lives, or stuck in a place where we have buried that desire to do more, be more, and leave a legacy because we have made our selves believe that this is just the way life is? When did we lie to ourselves and begin to believe that having a job that we don't like, being buried in debt and student loans, and never being able to keep up with the Jones' (but, by God, I'm going to try) is the status quo? When did this ugly status quo become a part of what's meant to be a beautiful life?

In true rebel fashion, I began to question the status quo. I began to follow the cry of my soul and dig until I started to unearth the message that was buried inside. I began to follow my heart and uncover my own strengths, gifts, abilities, likes, and dislikes. I made steps toward living fully alive in my true purpose.

I'll admit, even today as you read this, I haven't "arrived", nor will I ever. I believe that a person's purpose is something that evolves and grows as they do... but they must be willing to do the work, to unapologetically (and usually afraid), step into that purpose, despite what others may say or think or post or do. They have to authentically own it, as scary as it may be. Own our story, our mess, our faults, and our failures. Own your *human-ness* in all its capacity and be okay with it. Feel the fear, the anger, the jealousy, the self-doubt, the shame, the judgment and the not enough. Feel it, accept it as a part of being human, give that part of your soul some healing, give yourself a big dose of grace, and step into that next level of power and love.

I believe life is not only about owning the worst parts of us, but also owning the best parts. So many times, we can focus on the worst, the negative, the faults, and shortcomings that we forget that you *actually are* pretty amazing. I believe it's about owning that you *are* beautiful in every way. Owning that you *are* smart, powerful, kind, worthy, chosen, called, gifted, you are enough, and you have what it takes.

But how do we figure that out? How do you know what you've been "gifted" with as a human being? How do you know what is a talent, or a weakness, or something that you're just not even supposed to worry about? How do you sort through the things you aren't naturally good at compared to the things that you are? I'll try and explain. We tend to group "gifts and talents" together in the same obscure category. I don't know about you, but for me, this was always a little muddy. What the heck did it mean, that I was "gifted and talented?"

It was recently at the Women Ignite Conference, when one of the speakers explained it in a way I had never heard. It made total sense to me, so I'll share it with you, in hopes that if the waters are muddy for you in this area, this can give a little fresh insight.

Gifts are the things you have been good at your entire life. Imagine being a little kid... What were you naturally drawn to do, say, share, speak, read, etc.? Imagine being back in your childhood because that's back before you learned what society's standards were of you and began to act and do things according to those standards. If you look at a child, they are the true expression of what it means to be alive and in wonder of the world around you.

When I watch my son, Judah, the way he absorbs everything around him, reads books, learns words, studies people and faces, and watches everything, he is looking at the world as the new experience that it is to him. Even as a toddler, Judah is very mechanical and detail oriented. He loves hard like his mama and he lights up a room like his daddy. If you imagine being back in that childhood stage of your life, what did you love? What were you naturally good at? The things you didn't even have to try or practice or pretend to love? What did your soul feel "at home" in while you were doing it?

For me, I remember reading and writing all the time. I read books like crazy and wrote poetry and journaled all the time. I loved to be in front of a camera. Friends would come over for play dates and we would play "news." We would use my parent's HUGE (and when I say huge, I mean the size of a big diaper bag) home video camera, and we would pretend like we were newscasters. We would talk about the weather, we would joke together, and make a full show and production.

Maybe I should dig an old VHS up, get it converted to a digital video and upload it to my YouTube Channel. (Or maybe not!) Another thing that I loved and that came naturally to me when I was little was the ability to sing, be on stage, and share something with the audience in a microphone. I was comfortable. I felt at home and alive when I did. I guess it was a good thing that I was a part of a traveling dance, singing, and performance team all throughout my childhood.

People would come up to me and ask how come, even at such a young age, that I wasn't scared to share my story in the microphone or sing a solo in front of thousands of people. I just wasn't… It was a gift I was given. When I'm on stage, even to this day, the comfort and "alive-ness" I feel makes me feel like my soul is at home. I wasn't always comfortable with the feeling of being comfortable on stage though. I went through a period of time where I felt wrong for feeling alive on stage or when I wrote or sang. I felt selfish, self-absorbed, and like I should really just be a good quiet girl that didn't want the spotlight. This is where things can get tricky. This is the ugly side of having a beautiful gift. There will be an attempt, by the darkness, to have you not discover or claim your gifts.

I was a first-born child. Although I started out a little rough in the beginning, I was a natural leader. (I was a very bossy big sister... Sorry, brothers!) I naturally took charge in situations at school, I was often the team captain, and even in my college party days, I was given the nickname "mother hen" because I would always make sure my friends were close by and safe. I also loved creating and holding a space of depth and substance between friends (the actual friends who I allowed in) – a safe place where walls could come down, connections could be made, and souls could shine. I would bring people together and start to ask the deeper questions that drew out someone's hopes, dreams, and potential. I found that it's within that kind of space, we are truly human – in all our beautiful flaws, with no judgment, and we have permission to just be who we truly are. The assault on this gift of mine was receiving hurtful wounds, especially from women, and the close friends I did have, our tribes dissolved as we grew apart, moved, went to college, etc.

Another gift I was given is my beauty. God blessed me with an appearance that is aesthetically pleasing to today's standards of society. I used to think this was a mistake, and I didn't like looking or feeling pretty, much less actually admit it because well, "us women just shouldn't do that." I am finally at home with my authentic beauty, and I know that there is a reason for it (other than winning beauty pageants). I know that I am good in front of a still and video camera, and I can use these tools and this gift to share hope and life and light in a world that needs to know they are beautiful.

I will give this warning: when you begin to discover and own your God given gifts, like I mentioned, there are forces that will come against you and try to discourage you from using them. I am saying this because I have experienced this very thing and I have heard countless stories of other people experiencing this as well. Maybe you can look back, and as you start to recognize your gifts, you can also start to recognize where they have tried to be stifled and held back. Whether these forces are the hurtful words from others or the self-sabotaging thoughts you tell yourself, or even the truly dark spiritual forces that hold you back, they are real, and they will try and keep you from fiercely owning your true gifts.

When you start to fully and powerfully step into the gifts that God has given you, you become dangerous to the darkness. You and your light become so blinding to the darkness that it has no choice but to flee. You become a threat, and a very effective one at it, I might add. I used to really battle with feeling wrong for liking being in front of people or leading people, or singing or speaking life into someone's heart. I used to feel like I was wrong and selfish and narcissistic for wanting to do those things. I still hear those self-sabotaging thoughts that try and hold me back from writing or speaking or singing or creating courses or safe spaces for women to let down their guards and own their fierce beauty. I still get stuck. I still struggle. And that's okay. It's a process...

Now that we understand gifts a bit more, let's move on to talents. Talents are things that we have to work at. Now, it's not to say that we shouldn't and don't have to continue to refine and develop our natural gifts. It just means that refining our gifts will come easier than refining our talents. An example of a talent is cooking. Cooking, for some, may be a gift. When I was recently getting my nails done, I saw a kid's cooking show on TV. I was so impressed by these five-year-olds who whipped up these extravagant dishes with ingredients I've never even heard of, and they loved it. Cooking, for those kids, is a gift.

For me, cooking is *not* a gift. #dontjudge Now don't get me wrong, I can follow directions and a recipe will turn out great, but I'm not naturally gifted at cooking. I can't just whip up a gourmet meal with a dash of this and a pinch of that. I haven't done it enough for this talent to grow to the point where it feels natural and creative. Maybe one day I will develop my talent of cooking into something that comes more naturally, but for now, my husband is the chef, I take poopy-diaper duty, and we all eventually enjoy a great meal together.

Talents are the things and skills that you learn along the way. We tend to fumble through these, they are messy at first, and we have to get through the awkwardness of a learning curve. There is absolutely a place in your life for talents, so please don't just drop everything that you have to learn in life and only focus on your gifts. Learning and developing talents will be something that serves you for the rest of your life. An example of this is marketing and social media. I didn't always know how to market or use social media or blog or use YouTube. I had to learn. I had to get in the trenches, get my hands dirty, and fumble forward in the process. I had to do (and still do) a lot of things wrong before I started to get some of it right. I'm still no expert and there are always new technologies and strategies that come out, so staying on top of those things is the continued evolution of this talent.

Another great way to begin to understand your strengths, or "super-powers," as my good friend Sheli Gartman, CEO and Founder of Women Ignite, likes to say is by taking the Gallup StrengthsFinder Test. This is a ground-breaking test where you answer questions and it puts 34 different strengths in order. The amazing part about this test is that it "describes specific patterns of thought, feelings, or behavior that can be productively applied. These talents are specific enough to warrant their own definitions, their own expectations, and their own successful outcomes…Your strengths are listed in order of intensity, making the combination of your talents even more distinctive. If you wanted to find someone with the same top five themes in the same order as you, the odds are one in 33.4 million." (4)

This means that the strengths that you have, and the way that you can apply them to the world around you is unique to you. You are special. You were made to stand out from the crowd, and to use your superpowers in only the way that you can. I remember the first time I took the StrengthsFinder Test. After seeing what my top strengths were, it gave me permission to be "at home" in my strengths and not feel wrong for doing something a certain way or thinking a certain way. One of my top ten strengths is Positivity. Like I mentioned before, some people tried to tear me down for being "too positive." But guess what? Now that I know it's a strength of mine, it doesn't matter that they think I live in "Positivity La-La Land" and ride magical unicorns. I own and love the fact that it is a strength of mine to be able to see the best in a situation and to see and draw out the best in others. Another strength I have is called Maximizer. It means that I can take something that has good potential and make it great. I am confident in my ability to bring someone from good to great by seeing the potential inside of them. My "connectedness" strength allows me to be great at spiritually connecting people together and holding a space where they can be safe. Pair these with my other strategic strength and I can give steps on how to get to a desired outcome. Knowing these things about me is part of what makes me confident in my ability to lead, write, coach, facilitate workshops, develop community and create online courses. I was made for this, and my entire being feels alive and in alignment with my true self when I am functioning within these spaces where my strengths can shine through. I want to invite you to take the Gallup StrengthsFinders test by visiting CharityMajors.com/BeautifulResources and follow the link from this chapter.

I encourage you to take some time away from the noise, the social media, and the hustle and bustle and begin to sift through the things that are gifts and talents in your life. What were you naturally good at as a child? What did you love? What lit you up and gave you the authentic joy that you see on a child's face? Ask your family, ask your childhood friends, ask the child inside of you.

As you begin to pinpoint those things, I want to encourage you, if you aren't already, begin to incorporate those things into your life. It may look like taking piano lessons again or getting a new cookbook. It may mean volunteering with children or starting to host a group of friends once a month at your house, so you can connect and teach and create a safe space. It may mean you begin to write again or set aside money, so you can take that adventure you always wanted to.

Beginning to own your gifts means that you need to make space in your day and be intentional about incorporating those things in your life. It won't happen on accident and you may experience some resistance as you begin to bring back the joy and light into your life. It's okay. And guess what? #youareworthit Your light, your gifts, you fully alive and in alignment with why you are here on this planet, is needed in this world. We need you - all of you - in all of your brightness, unapologetically shining for others to see. Everyone is waiting for someone else to go first, so be brave. #gofirst Do the thing, create the thing, write the thing, or build the thing. Whatever it is. Whatever gifts you have been given, use them. The world is waiting...

Chapter 9
Bring on the Arrows

Arrows, darts, and death by a thousand cuts - all sound torturous and not very fun. Unfortunately, as we have learned in this book and through experiences in life, wounds, big and small, happen. We are human, we are messy, we won't always get it right, and neither will those around us. It's important to understand this common knowledge…and not just know it but also truly understand it at a core level.

Studies show that the human brain likes things to connect and make sense of things. When something doesn't make sense, brain activity amps up and fills in the blanks along the way. The "blanks" are based on that individual's past experiences and subconscious understanding of the world around them.

Here is an example. Imagine being in a house, and a dog comes running through the door. He is soaking wet, dripping all over the floor. The dog comes running around the corner in the house, brushes against your leg, shakes the water off, heads towards his water bowl and begins to drink.

Now I'll ask you: what kind of dog was it? What color was the floor of the house? What kind of pants were you wearing when the dog rubbed up against your leg? What type of water bowl was it?

As your brain filled in the parts of this story, it is based on your past experiences. Maybe you saw a golden retriever dog or a lab or a yorkie or your childhood dog. Maybe the floor of the house was carpet to one person but to someone else, it is hardwood. Some people picture themselves wearing jeans, some picture slacks, and if you're my son, I'm pretty sure he would picture himself in just a diaper because he loves to be free of clothes. Was the water bowl metal or wood or plastic or some other type of bowl that you have seen somewhere?

See how we can take the same story, but because of all of our different life experiences as individual humans, our brain fills in the blanks differently? This is a big reason why people misunderstand each other, especially when it comes to different beliefs, skin colors, political sides, backgrounds, and what we post on social media. Can you see how this brain operation can become an ugly side of being beautiful?

I was meeting with a new client who was going through one of my BeYOUty Revolution Transformations. She was excited and ready to step into a new level of confidence, get equipped with tools to help her dial up the beauty she possessed – inside and out. When we met, she admitted something to me. She admitted that she was scared to meet with me but it wasn't because of who I was. It was because of who I represented. Because of my looks, to her, I represented the "popular girls" in high school that teased her, hurt her and rejected her. She understood that it wasn't who I was that brought up these feelings, but it was because of her past experiences. My internal monologue said, "Oh great, apparently I represent rejection to everyone around me because of the "mean girls" in high school… grrreeeeaaattttt… that explains a lot…" (Side note - Ladies, can we change this stereotype? What if the pretty girls were also the nice girls? What if *all* girls were confident, loving, beautiful, and encouraging? What a beautiful world that would be…) I thanked my client for her honesty, but it also got me thinking. How many times do we put someone we don't even know, into a certain box or category, just because they trigger something in us that was in a past experience? What boxes have I put others in? And what boxes was I being put in by others based on their past experiences? This became a big #ahamoment for me and I began to understand the power of perception. Oh, our beautiful brains and how they fill in the blanks…

The unfortunate part about our brains doing this is that the story it fills in is based on our past experience (remember the dog running through the house example?), which is damaged and never perfect. The story we tell ourselves is usually the worst story possible instead of giving the person the benefit of the doubt. Have you ever called or texted someone and they didn't get back to you? What was the story you started to tell yourself? Are they mad at me? What did I do? They don't like me. #blahblahblah. In light of this knowledge, I propose this question: if our brains are going to make up a story anyways, what happens if we were to tell ourselves a different story? What if we were to believe the best about the other person (and ourselves) instead of the opposite?

My husband gets minor bursts of road rage when he drives. The stories he comes up with about the other drivers are sometimes comical and other times very "interesting." Not too long ago, we were driving to one of our favorite vacation spots. The road that leads up to the mountains is pretty narrow and windy. There are a few passing lanes, but for the most part, drivers tend to file in behind each other and hunker down for the curvy ride ahead. On this trip, there were a few cars following close to each other. Behind my cute white Acura mom-car, that my husband was driving, was a big black pickup truck, with lifted tires, tinted windows, and a loud engine.

A few cars, including us, were playing the "wait for the passing lane and floor it" game to pass a few slower cars and this big pickup truck behind us was doing the same. We finally made it to the front of the line, with the pickup close behind. At the next passing lane, the pickup floored it, the engine blasted through the mountain canyon, and they pulled up next to us, trying to pass. In the other lane ahead of us, a car came around the corner; the pickup saw them, slowed back down and pulled in behind us again.

My husband's eyes bugged out a bit and he began to say how big of an idiot that guy was, how his big truck was compensating for "something" that was smaller, and how he was going to get out of the car and have some choice words with the guy in the pickup. I laughed. I couldn't help it. I questioned why he was taking it so personally… I thought he was just trying to pass. Sure, maybe it was louder because of whatever fancy muffler was on the truck, but for some reason, my husband took offense and wanted to kick the guy's butt.

A few more curves in the road and another passing lane, the truck behind us floored it again and passed safely and loudly. The pickup driver got the stare of death from my husband, who I'm sure if he could, would have shot laser beams out of his eyeballs and blown up the big black truck. I laughed again, as this time, Chris began to make up another story about how the guy was a huge jerk, how he probably wasn't very smart and never graduated high school or driver's education for that matter, and mumbled a bit more about big tires and big trucks overcompensate for tiny "things." I laughed it off, told him to relax, and I changed the subject.

Although I'm no psychologist and I'm definitely not my husband's "breakthrough buddy" (he can get his own therapist for that), I wondered what was it about that truck that made my husband feel insecure or threatened and feel the need to lash out in a way that made him feel better about himself. Was it the loudness of the engine? The big tall black grill in the rearview mirror? Was it the tinted windows that guarded the true identity of the other driver?

How many people around us seem like the "big black truck?" Are there people who are really loud and proud? Or people who just seem to grill you all the time? What about people who hide in the shadows or keep masks up and you can never truly connect with their human spirit on the other side? Do you begin to put them down? Make assumptions about them as a person? Call them names and make them less threatening in your mind by telling yourself they are compensating for something?

Unfortunately, as human beings, we ALL do this. We all throw darts and arrows and sometimes laser beams from our eyeballs at others around us when we feel threatened or inferior. It's a natural response to protect yourself and make the other person feel inferior in your own mind. Especially when someone is in the public eye...

As a public figure and a community activist, everything I do, say, wear, write, and post is under a microscope. That is the cost of being in the public eye and being an influential person in a community. The interesting thing I find about being a leader is that leaders also tend to be targets. They tend to be who people judge the quickest, who gets criticized the most, and whose actions are often misunderstood or mis-perceived.

During my pursuit to Mrs. America, I had posted a little video in a business Facebook group. I was in between appointments, had a quick little commute, and needed to ask businesses for some silent auction items for a non-profit event. Having my headphones in and having a dashboard phone holder (since I like to practice safety and not hold the phone while I drive), I pushed record and recorded a cute little video and posted it at the next red light.

Little did I know that my "recording while driving" post would create a frenzy. People began to criticize me for not being a safe driver, for being a bad example to children, and that I shouldn't be looked at as a role model. One gentleman, in particular, took it upon himself to shame me as much as he could by contacting every news station, every newspaper, and posting about how bad of a person I was on many social media professional pages and Facebook groups. These things really hurt me because in all my "good and safe intention," I thought I had done the right thing. I had the phone dash-holder, I kept both hands on the wheel, I kept my eyes on the road, I used the headphones, and didn't feel any different as if I was talking to someone next to me in the car. But I had to take a step back and look at it objectively. Every leader and influencer needs to at one point or another.

Yes, as a public figure, everything I do is an example to others. It wasn't the best of examples to record a video while driving, and I should have chosen a better time to do it. I swallowed my pride, took down the post and publicly apologized. Then I began to wonder why this one man was so adamant about attacking me all over the place. Seek to understand first, before being understood, right? After some Googling and Facebook stalking, I found out that a distracted driver had injured one of his family members in a car accident. I suddenly saw what it was like to be in his shoes and understood where his passion was coming from. It made a lot more sense and began to seek ways to turn a negative situation around.

From my heart felt vulnerability and apology came more support, prayers, love and encouragement than I could have imagined. I was also able to turn a bad situation around by being proactive, connecting with the Department of Transportation and a few news stations and co-promote a movement against distracted driving. It was a good reminder that I *am* an example, I *am* a leader, and I *am* held to a higher standard. And I need to be okay with that. I need to be okay with having a microscope on what I do, and I also need to be strong enough to take the arrows that will undoubtedly come my way. It comes with the territory, and if I let myself, it can be something that keeps me playing small. Or I can accept the calling that is on my life to be an influencer and a public servant, and hold myself to that higher standard. It hasn't always been this way though…

Throughout my life, I have experienced dart after dart, laser beam after laser beam, and judgment after judgment. So much so, that there was a time in my life where I was scared to even do anything or say anything to other people because everyone around me seemed to be misinterpreting me completely. I began to play small, keep to myself, and walk on eggshells in fear of anyone misjudging whom I was and accusing me of something I didn't do or say. It was like no matter what I did, their brain "filled in the spaces" of my life and who I was as a person with the worst-case scenario. And every time it happened, it boggled my mind, hurt my feelings, and caused me to dim my light even more. My light was under heavy attack.

I have been accused of implying that my husband was better than another girls' husband because I posted a picture on Facebook of flowers that my husband got me. I have been accused of trashing another girl's personal core religious beliefs and attacking her as a person with a live video that I did about eating healthy things like fruits, vegetables and lean organic meats. I have been given nicknames like Volleyball Barbie because I wore a ribbon in my ponytail, Mrs. Potato Head when I was Mrs. Idaho, selfish, a narcissist, little Miss Perfect, greedy, manipulative, stupid, conceded, and Mrs. Positivity that lives in "Positivity-La-La Land".

Not the prettiest of pictures about a person, huh? What hurts the most is that these things, these accusations, these judgments, couldn't be farther from the truth. They are so uncharacteristic of me, who I am, how I was raised, how I treat people, and my core beliefs that it boggles my mind how someone could even think or say things like that about another person. And then I remember the power of perception, and how our brain fills in the blanks. I begin to feel empathy and compassion towards that person who is shooting arrows at me because in reality, they are hurting and I am the target of their hurt. I invite you to begin to see those who have thrown arrows at you in the same way. There is something about you that triggers something in them and once you can understand that what they see in you is actually what's going on within them, it changes everything. It did for me. It helped me step out of victim mode and into a mindset of compassion for that other person. It helped me to know how to pray for them, and to take time to check myself, my actions, my intentions, and how others may perceive them. I am not, nor will I ever be perfect…no one will…we will all mess up, we wont get something right, and that's ok. It is our job to do the best we can with what we have.

My favorite book says that "no weapon formed against me will prosper," but it doesn't say that there will be no weapons that are formed. That's the ugly side of having a beautiful calling on your life. Although they wont prosper, weapons will be formed.

So even in my good intentions and solid character, arrows have been thrown at my character, my integrity, and who I am as a leader. Those are the arrows that hurt me the most. I can handle if someone calls me a silly name or says my hair looks bad or they don't like my clothes (at least now I can). It's when someone makes a remark about *who I am* that really hurts. I know I'm not a bad person. I know that I genuinely love people and would do anything for others. I am loyal to a fault; I am generous, fun loving, easy-going, confident, passionate and driven. I know that I'm not perfect, and that I'm trying my best. And I believe that others are too.

It took me a long time, a lot of work, and a ton of personal development to start to stand firm in who I was, not play small and not worry about what others may say. I'll admit, it still hurts my feelings if someone says something negative about me, but I'm getting stronger and stronger every day and try and pray for that person instead of letting my mind shoot laser beams back at them. I'll admit something else to you... I'm scared, even as I write this book, that people will throw arrows and darts at me for sharing my story, for being vulnerable, for challenging you to grow, for shining a light on a topic that isn't talked about much. It's scary to "put it all out there" for the world to see and read and judge and fill in their own blanks.

The negative voices in my head scream loud and clear and say, "who do you think you are," "they're never going to like this," "you're not a good enough writer," "they are going to judge you even more..." It's scary, but I know I need to do it. Not for me (well, partially for me), but mostly for the one girl's life that this book might encourage. The one girl's heart that needs to hear that she is beautiful. The one woman's purpose she has not yet stepped into because she has been ridiculed like I have been. The light that has been dimmed and the heart that has the wounds from taking arrows. It's for you. It's for me. It's scary, but I know I must share it anyways.

As I lean into the fear, despite the negative voices swirling around in my head, I know I must keep writing and keep shining a light because we, as human beings, need to walk through the healing of the things we keep hidden in the dark. The first step to this is awareness. So here I am, flashlight in hand, scared out of my mind, and sharing these words in hope that we, as a human race, can all begin to move toward believing the best about others. Truly loving one another in our unique beauty, instead of throwing arrows and darts at one another in hopes that the other person won't threaten our existence. I believe in a world where a woman's beauty is not a threat to another woman. I believe in a world where, when someone does something new, her friends don't try and tear her down for it. I believe in a world where our flaws and failures are actually what make us perfect. I believe in a world where masks are trampled on by the power of vulnerability and authenticity. I believe in a world where men are not threatened by a woman who has fully owned her greatness. I believe in a world where women champion other women, where we collaborate instead of compete, and where we truly embrace the fierce power that is within us to make the world a beautifully better place.

In a perfect world (which I know doesn't exist on this side of eternity), that's what it would be like. It would be like nature – like a field of wildflowers – where one flower isn't intimidated by the blooming of another flower next to it. They all just bloom – in all their brilliance... together...beautifully together. But since we are on this side of eternity, we need to understand that arrows will come, darts will be thrown, laser beams will be shot out of judgmental eyes, and we pretty much have to get stronger and be okay with it.

We (myself included), cannot play small, can't "say the thing" or "do the thing" or "create the thing" in fear that someone will judge us. It's going to happen regardless, so go BIG, Girl. Hold yourself to a higher standard and go BIG, go all out, go for it, do it afraid, and shine brighter than ever before. Arrows and all. We are strong enough. You are strong enough.

So shine, Beautiful One.

Chapter 10
Why, Yes, I'll Have Another Bottle of Wine

Despite how awesome things look on the outside, I've been there. I've experienced the deepest low of what it means to literally not get out of bed or have the desire to go on. I've been at the point of numbing myself with a bottle of wine. It felt better than the present pain of being aware that I didn't even have the energy to think, pray, smile, get up out of bed, or do anything but stare at the wall. The truth is, that I wasn't alone, even though it felt that way. Almost 15 million people in the United States suffer from depression.

Depression can be caused by a multitude of things, especially today where it is so easy to scroll through social media and see all the highlight reels of everyone else's lives, all the while we are in sweat pants, haven't showered, the house is a mess and it's Friday night. *Awesome. I'm such a party animal!*

For me, my depression set in after coming out of a position that fueled my deeper purpose. I had been a public figure of sorts for the term of the year that I was assigned, and felt more alive during that year than I had in a long time. I was thriving in the community, I was in leadership positions, and I was getting recognition that made me feel good. I was growing, leading, learning, and loving it.

I understood the position was only for a year, so I wanted to make the most out of it. Having done a lot during that time in terms of community service, networking, growing influence, etc., I also tried to prepare myself for the end of it (or so I thought). I either hadn't prepared enough or I didn't know the extent of how far down I would sink. I figured there would be a natural "low" after such a high point, but why had I sunk so far? This natural correction of energy is the ugly side of a beautiful high in life…or is it?

During my "low," I knew it would be good for me to pray, but I didn't even have the energy to open my mouth. I knew it would be good to read, but I didn't have the mental capacity to comprehend what I was reading. I knew it would be good to listen to inspiring podcasts, but my fingers wouldn't do anything else but mindlessly scroll through social media for hours on end.

There was an interesting internal battle going on. My conscious mind knew that it was a phase - I would come out, I was stronger, I knew what would help snap me out of it and God had a big purpose still in store. But my subconscious wouldn't let me move or act on any of those promises I believed in or any of the actions that would allow me to begin to climb out.

I never felt so internally conflicted and purpose-less. I had gone through struggles before when I had graduated college. I had put so much of my identity in my position as a volleyball player that when it went away, I didn't know whom I was or what I was a part of. This time, it felt different. I was conscious of not allowing my identity to be wrapped up in the public position I held.

Was it that I didn't know what was next? Why is it when you are weak that the negative self-talk that keeps you down becomes the loudest? Why is it when you need a "pick-me-up" the most that your mind keeps you down, plays tricks on you, and tells you lies?

Had I taken the time to seek and plan out what's next or had the answer not come to me yet? Did I miss the answer? I knew I was bored with my profession as a trainer and the couple of clients that I had were still hanging on for dear life (truth be told, they came more for the therapy and friendship than they did for the actual workout).

Was that it? That was all that I was going to amount to and that was going to be the best year of my life and it was all-downhill from there? Geez, I hoped not but the negative thoughts kept coming. "You're all washed up now. That was the best you will ever amount to. You missed out on so many opportunities. You didn't do enough. You didn't serve enough. You didn't make the connections you needed to make. You are washed up. You shouldn't even get out of bed. What's the use of getting out of bed? You're not getting up to do anything. Here, have another glass of wine. Let's scroll and look at everyone else's happy amazing lives while you lay here in your funk…".

Truth be told, wine and mindlessly scrolling through social media were the only things that would shut my brain up. Normally, I'm a happy, positive, mentally strong person. What happened in the span of a day? Where had these thoughts come from? Certainly, they weren't buried below the surface in the depths of my subconscious? If so, why were they there? Who put them there? And why were they all coming up at once?

It's in the pressure of life that you experience what's truly below the surface. It's kind of like the process of making wine. You don't get wine unless you squeeze the juice out of the grapes. But it's a messy process. It's a process that requires pressure, filtering, mixing, sanitizing, growth, isolation, suffocation, adjustments, and enjoying. Let me explain…

I'm no wine maker, although I do like to enjoy a glass or two here and there (not full bottles anymore). I like to visit wineries for their delicious tapas, scenery, and wine tasting, and I started to learn a little bit about the process of making wine. It's a bit like life, as you will find.

To make wine, certain equipment is needed. Things like jars, buckets, mesh, corks, mixing utensils, etc. There are also certain ingredients needed. Grapes, sugar, water and yeast. The process begins by choosing your grapes, washing them, and crushing them to get the juice out. Isn't it just like life to give you certain "equipment" like your gifts and purpose, having to mix them with certain "ingredients" like your talents, your experiences and people around you, and then comes the cleansing and pressure process.

But back to the wine… after the crushing and pressure comes the filtering. The juice of the grapes gets mixed up with the pulp, so to get the pure juice that makes the wine, the "junk" or the unwanted parts of the grape must be ran through a filtering cloth so that all that remains is the juice. Once the juice is mixed with sugar, water, and yeast, it is set aside to ferment and be turned into the deliciousness that we call wine.

It's kind of like the part of your journey when you go through something hard. The pressure brings out the juiciness of who you are, but it also brings out some of the junk. It is up to you to filter through the junk and add in the right ingredients that cause you to sweetly grow (like the yeast and sugar in the wine).

It's up to you to use the times of being alone, like wine on a shelf, to brew your best ideas, to sift through the habits, thoughts, things, and people in your life that are no longer for your best and highest good, because there may not be room for them where you are going. Once you are ready to serve others, you can do so to the best of your abilities. Just like when a great glass of wine is served, life is meant to be enjoyed, and enliven the senses through the experience of taste and aroma. It helps you let down your guard, enjoy the moment, and make good conversations and connect with others.

So, what did I do after I snapped out of my wine funk? I volunteered my time at places that I knew would make me grateful for where I was and everything that I had. I got involved at women's shelters and homeless shelters. I worked with teens and their emotional intelligence. I began to use the down time to brew my best ideas. That's where some of these chapters have come from, where my speaking training started, where I was able to dive into leadership courses, business masterminds, and entrepreneur trainings. I used the downtime to slow down, listen to my heart and the voice of Truth about me, who I was, and where God was taking me. The title for this book actually came from that time! Oh, and we made a baby! The downtime turned into the greatest gift because I was able to focus on having a healthy, calm, stress-free pregnancy, and I have no doubt that's why my son is such a happy and well-mannered kid. He grew in an environment full of love and care, not one full of stress and worry. What a gift that season of life turned out to be. I found the juiciness of life in what started out as a bottle of wine.

Maybe you, like me, have experienced that deep depression, or discontentment or you're not quite sure who you are meant to be or what you're supposed to do. Although it is still a hard process to be in the middle of and it's always easier to say, "invite the wine-making process" into your life so that you can serve others at the next level of your purpose. *After* it's over, if you find yourself reaching for that bottle of wine, remember this analogy, put down the bottle and start to do the work on yourself. I also want to encourage you to give, volunteer and serve, even if it's volunteering at your local homeless shelter. There is nothing like serving others that snaps a person out of their funk, makes them grateful for where they are, and gets them back on track going towards their mission.

I want to encourage you to embrace the pressure and the purification process. For it's within that time that the juiciness of who you are, and the purpose God has on your life will come out. Embrace the pressure. Embrace the cleansing. Embrace the process of growth. It's all a part of your journey and your purpose.

Chapter 11
A Magic Wand Life

As we near the end of this book, I hope you have found some value as I shared my story, some of what I believe can make the world a better place, and how I believe in the potential and God given purpose that is inside of you.

I have one last exercise I'd like for you to do with me.

Imagine I have a magic wand...

I have a magic wand, and as you are reading this, I am waving it. All sorts of glitter and sparkles and unicorn sprinkles are sweetly dusting you and your life. You now have *all* of the money and *all* of the time in the world. #jackpot

The question I have for you is this: What would you *really* be doing with your life?

I want you to take a moment and really think about this. Maybe even journal about it. There are no right or wrong answers, and nothing is out of reach.

If you want to:
Travel to the moon
Build the largest art museum
Take a trip around the world with your family
Give trillions of dollars to save children trapped in the sex slave industry
Invent the next piece of technology that will forever change the world

Hire a chef and a massage therapist and a hair-dresser every day of the week (that's one of mine)…
Nothing *is out of reach.*

What would you *really* be doing with your life? How would you spend your time and your unlimited resources? Who would be there with you? How would you feel?

Dream and journal for a bit… Then keep reading…

As I have asked this question, I've found that most people don't allow themselves to dream this big. Most people say they would pay off their credit card, go on vacation for a couple weeks, and that's about it. They literally stop their brain and imagination from getting any bigger. Why is this? When did we lose the imagination we had when we were young when we could be anything we ever wanted? When the world wasn't such a serious place and we could run around with no pants on and nobody cared. When we walked up to random people and started conversations about our poop, how good the food was at snack time, how our daddy caught us from the monkey bars, how our Barbies were all friends, and about how we just built a rocket ship out of pillows that was going to take us to the moon because that's what was going on in our lives.

I began to ask this question because someone had once asked me, and I found that I hadn't allowed myself to dream big. As I mentioned before, I had settled for what my current reality was and "hoped that one day" the big dreams that I had buried deep in my heart would one day come true. I had settled for waking up, going to work, going to the grocery store and wandering the aisles, living for the weekends, posting about TGIF, hump-day Wednesdays, Throwback Thursdays, and barely making enough to pay my bills, chip away at the mountain of student loans, and Monday would roll back around. I had settled for the grind. My "truth" (with a lower-case t, compared to a universal Truth with a capital "T") was Groundhog Day, where I would maybe get a vacation a year, a stay-cation if I was lucky, and the reality that the dreams I had when I was younger about being an author, a speaker, a world-traveler, a difference maker, and a potential igniter were just too farfetched and not realistic.

When did we stop believing that we could go, do, create, be, say, and have wherever we dreamed? When did the carefree spirit of the little girl on the playground who didn't have a care in the world?

Maybe you, like me, have felt that same way about life. Maybe you have been playing small, too, and settling for the status quo. Maybe you have said "someday", too. It's okay. This ugly side of this beautiful thing we call life has hope… But, there's a trick…

The dreams that I had buried for so long are still being uncovered and some of them still seem like a long way off (like starting an orphanage or a center that rescues women and children out of human-trafficking or working with women to build their self-confidence and their beauty, inside and out, and yes, having a hair dresser do my hair. (Every. Single. Day). #itwillhappen #goals

Although I am still working toward those things that I see on my vision board and in the big crazy dreams I see in my head, I now know that I am not limited by my current reality or what I can see that's just in front of me. I am only limited by *me*, and I'm working on getting myself out of the way so that I can be used to make an impact on the world… not for the sake of me doing something great, but for the sake of living a life that will leave something that will outlive me. For the sake of the lives and hearts that will be changed so they can help change the world.

THIS is what it's all about. This is the beautiful journey of what we call life. It is your purpose to find your purpose and to live it out… fully, fiercely, and brightly.

I want to challenge you to do this exercise and begin to unpack the hopes and dreams that are inside of you. It may take you quite a few times to begin to allow your brain to follow the unlimited possibilities of dreaming this big. Get a journal, and write it down. Nothing is too big, nothing is too farfetched. Nothing is wrong, and nothing is out of reach. Dream, Darling, for "as you dream, so shall you be."

There will be some sifting and sorting of these dreams and visions that goes on and you may begin to question, which dreams are the ones for me? Which dream has been buried in my heart, and how do I know it's what I'm supposed to pursue? Whenever you have been given a dream, it is placed deep within your heart. The Hebrew word for "heart" (or *kardiva)*, literally means "the real you." Ancient writings use the word, "heart" to mean your love, your internal motivation, and your passions. When you have a God given passion for something, it literally means it is incorporated within your being. It is a part of you, and your story. Your mess becomes your message, and it's one worth telling. The places you fear exposure, the places you hold most sacred and protect their vulnerability, that's where your power lies. That's where the dreams are stored.

"The brightest candle gives off the biggest shadow." It's the places of your shadow that will bring out the brightest light, and give you the flame to ignite others.

As you begin to dream bigger and ignite what is within you, I have one more challenge for you. I want to challenge you to write a letter to your future self. Write yourself a letter, one that you will read one year from now, five years from now, and even ten years from now. Write it to yourself, in present and past tense (not future tense), saying how grateful you are for having done _____ and for having _____ in your life. List how the accomplishments you have done, the things and people you have in your life, how you are feeling, and the mindset you are coming from. Write it as if these things have already come to pass. After you write those letters to yourself, seal them and write the date you want to open them. Keep them in a safe place (but not the safe place that you forget about where they are at). Keep those letters in mind and begin to implement your gifts and talents, daily habits, tasks, goals and actions that will move you towards what is within those letters. And remember that the beauty is within the journey of what will get you towards what is written within those pages.

Another beautiful thing is now you are aware, you have grown in your consciousness of what your life can become, who you desire to grow into and how you can choose to move towards it. You have officially been commissioned. Chosen. Anointed. Called. You now know some tools and resources. You now have a tribe and a coach that believes in you and the potential that is inside of you, just waiting to be ignited. You cannot play small. You cannot stay dimmed. Regardless of what anyone else may say. Regardless of what the chattering voices within you may tell you. The world needs you. We need you. I need you. The lives of those you will impact need you. We need your strength, your light, your love, and your story. You are a piece to this puzzle we call life and it wouldn't be complete without you. You must shine.

It's up to you now, Beautiful One. Claim your beauty, your power, your light, your purpose and your story - wholeheartedly, fully, and unapologetically. Inspire and ignite others to shine as well. Choose to see the best in them and in yourself, have fun, and be YOU. Because you are here for such a time as this and that is the beauty of it all...

People are often unreasonable, irrational, and self-centered.
Forgive them anyway.
If you are kind, people may accuse you of selfish ulterior motives.
Be kind anyway.
If you are successful, you'll win some unfaithful friends and some genius enemies.
Succeed anyway.
If you are honest and sincere people may deceive you.
Be honest and sincere anyway.
What you spend years creating, others could destroy overnight.
Create anyway.
If you find serenity and happiness, some may be jealous.
Be happy anyway.
The good you do today will often be forgotten.
Do good anyway.
Give the best you have, and it will never be enough.
Give your best anyway.
In the final analysis, it is between you and God.
It was never between you and them anyway.
– Mother Teresa

#THEUGLYSIDEOFBEINGBEAUTIFUL
@CHARITYMAJORS

References

(1) http://www.healthguidance.org/entry/16417/1/Physical-Traits-That-Are-Universally-Attractive-in-Men-and-Women.html)

(2) http://innertranquility.com.au

(3) (https://nobullying.com/cyber-bullying-statistics-2014/)

(4) http://coaching.gallup.com/2013/08/.

About Charity Majors

As a Speaker, Author, Podcaster, Entrepreneur, Life Transformation Specialist, Fitness and Nutrition Expert, and former Pageant Winner, Charity Majors speaks life into the hearts of those who are ready to ignite their life and unapologetically take their body, beauty, business, and life to the next level.

Her two favorite titles are Mom to her son, Judah and Wife to her husband, Chris. Charity and her family call Boise, Idaho, their home base. You can also find them cozying up in their tiny house in the mountains or adventuring all around the world, exploring above and below the ocean.

Charity is available for speaking, coaching, and has her online courses available to empower you and your tribe to own your beauty, inside and out. Visit CharityMajors.com.

This book is proudly published by WIPublish,
A Division of Women Ignite International.

Contact: Terilee Harrison, Director WIPublish
terilee@womenigniteinternational.com

Find us online: www.womenigniteinternational.com
LIKE us on Facebook: www.Facebook.com/wipublish

27238597R00066

Made in the USA
Lexington, KY
28 December 2018